# The Evolution and Destruction

## of the

# Original Electoral College

### Third Edition – April 2013

Expanded with additional Quotes and Index

This work provides an in-depth analysis of the ingenious system that the Framers designed to identify the best possible presidential candidates.

\* \* \*

Unfortunately the system has been destroyed by the machinations of party politics. All patriots interested in restoring the Framers' original plan will recognize the need to understand this unique process.

# The Evolution and Destruction

## of the

# Original Electoral College

### Including an examination of *Federalist No. 68*
### (Alexander Hamilton Defends the Electoral College)

> When people ask us "How could this country create a system which would consistently produce high quality presidents?" our answer is:
> **"Focus on the quality of the candidates."**

Gary and Carolyn Alder
Freedom Coaches

A system that only produces the best candidates will always produce the best presidents. Of course this is true for all elected positions, but if we can sell the idea for choosing presidents the rest will follow.

The Evolution and Destruction of the Original Electoral College
Copyright © 2010 Gary & Carolyn Alder
Second Edition - 2011 - ISBN-13:978-1-4609-7941-9
Third Edition   - 2013 - ISBN-13:978-0-9828237-2-9

ALL RIGHTS RESERVED.  No part of this book may be reproduced in any manner whatsoever without written permission of the publisher, except for brief quotations in articles and reviews.

Published by Advance Freedom, LLC
c/o Carolyn Alder
P.O. Box 306
Cokeville, WY  83114
books@freedomformula.us
(307) 279-0287   (801) 599-9819 (cell)

Gary and Carolyn Alder are dedicated to teaching the principles of freedom.  This passion takes form in producing and delivering classes, lectures and written articles about freedom in the religious, economic and political realms of our lives.

Gary is a retired computer programmer/analyst and so has a natural and professional interest in organizing component parts to match a predetermined plan or system.  Carolyn is interested in sharing the specific words of the Founders and Framers.  Their words provide a window to look into their hearts and minds.

This work is created on the premise that the Framers of the Constitution were designing a system to establish and maintain the freedoms and rights described in the Declaration of Independence.

For an in-depth study of the United States Constitution, the paradigm of the Founders, and the principles of freedom in the religious, economic, and political realms visit:  ***www.FreedomFormula.us***

USA "Best Books 2011" Award Winner
    Government/Political Science category

Cover Design by Paul Flinn

Printed in the United States of America

# *What Others Have to Say*

"As a constitutional attorney, I thought I understood the Electoral College pretty well. But in their excellent book *The Evolution and Destruction of the Original Electoral College*, Gary and Carolyn Alder have given me a thorough education. Our Founding Fathers created a constitutional republic in which the States, and the people only indirectly, choose the President. But through a series of amendments and implementing legislation, the Framers' intent is being undermined and the constitutional republic they designed is being transmuted into a people's democracy in which the national government is supreme and the states are merely administrative subdivisions. In *The Evolution and Destruction of the Original Electoral College*, the Alders have sounded a call to arms and have provided an arsenal of information that gives patriots the ammunition they need to reverse this trend and restore our republic. 'Must reading' for defenders of our Constitution."

> —**John A. Eidsmoe**, Colonel, Alabama State Defense Force
> Professor, Oak Brook College of Law & Government Policy
> Senior Counsel & Scholar-in-Residence, Foundation for Moral Law

"Gary and Carolyn Alder have done a magnificent job researching the Electoral College to produce a new book titled *The Evolution and Destruction of the Original Electoral College*. Their work clearly shows how the Framers intended this new Republic to choose its leader, and why the leader should be chosen indirectly rather than by a direct vote of the people. The authors support their conclusions with evidence from the Framers themselves, from the Constitution, from the *Federalist Papers*, and many other sources. They identify the 12th Amendment in 1804 as the beginning of the end for the Electoral College, and trace how over two centuries political parties have taken control and completely destroyed the original concept. The process now in place is not authorized by the Constitution, but no one knows it. This information is not taught in schools, but it should be. Every American should read this import book and begin the process to return to the America our Framers created."

> —**Henry Lamb**, Executive VP, Freedom 21
> Chair, Sovereignty International
> Columnist, author of *The Rise of Global Governance*

"What is the Electoral College and what has happened to it? *The Evolution and Destruction of the Original Electoral College* is an elaboration of what the Electoral College is, its purpose, and how its spirit has been corrupted in the modern day by political parties throughout history. A worthwhile read that describes the electoral process as a whole and what needs to be known about the problems that we face today, *The Evolution and Destruction of the Original Electoral College* is a worthy read for those seeking political understanding in today's world."

    **—James A. Cox** – Editor-in-Chief
        Midwest Book Review

"I was intrigued by your management of the topic and set all other reading aside to study the content. I have seen nothing like it. This work on the Electoral College will fill an important void and aid many people to overcome the region of ignorance in which we all seem to wallow to some degree. Also I rejoice in your steady commitment in promoting the cause of liberty. There seems to be an awakening interest in the topic."

    **—Stephen Pratt** – Constitutional Scholar and Lecturer
        Founder of *Know Your Liberty*
        www.libertyandlearning.com

"The best candidates for President rarely rise to electability because America fell into the European trap. It came with the 12th amendment that engrained the inefficient European two-party model into America's election process. This divisive change twisted our nation's presidential election process from choosing the best of the best into a $2 billion beauty pageant. That road to ruin is clearly explained in Gary and Carolyn Alder's delightful analysis entitled *The Evolution and Destruction of the Original Electoral College*. In their well-sourced description they explain the Electoral College's origins, purpose, and demise. They also give hope and solutions for how we can and must return to that winning formula. This is *must* reading for Americans of all ages left wondering who hijacked our presidential election process and how to get it back."

    **—Paul B. Skousen** (son of W. Cleon Skousen)
        National Constitution Coach
        Former intelligence officer in the CIA and the Reagan
        White House

"Your understanding of the original electoral college is the same as mine. ...Madison assumed that presidential elections would end up in the House of Representatives 'nineteen out of twenty times'– just what you say on page 33. [page 62 in this edition] ... I found your booklet well written and informative and enjoyed reading it. My only questions have to do with the 'value judgments.' I believe you are performing a wonderful educational function and one that will make the participants in your programs better citizens (and maybe even better people)."

—**John V. Orth**
William Rand Kenan, Jr. Professor of Law
University of North Carolina

"I have read and then re-read your book, *The Evolution and Destruction of the Original Electoral College.* This is a subject that I have studied for years and I have great interest in it. You have taken a very complex issue to explain and made it very easy to understand. I share your views and concerns that we have truly walked away from the original Electoral College as formulated by our Founders."

—**"Senator Bob" Smith** – Former US Senator – New Hampshire

"In these days when our freedom is in such grave danger I am pleased to see Gary and Carolyn Alder's book on the electoral college which explains the Founders' great effort to protect against the influence of party politics in the selection of a president and vice president and what it has become over the years."

—**Jerome Horowitz** – author of:
*The Elders of Israel and the Constitution*
*The United States Has Two Constitutions*

"Once again, it shows how the Founders' original formula would solve many problems today. Understanding the Founders' wisdom in choosing a president is a vital step in restoring the Constitution. There is still a lot of teaching to be done!"

—**Earl Taylor, Jr.** – President, National Center for Constitutional Studies (NCCS)
NCCS featured Alders book in the NCCS November 2010 Newsletter www.nccs.net/newsletter/nov10nl.html

"*The Evolution and Destruction of the Original Electoral College* is an in-depth analysis of how we should elect our Presidents. The Framers of our Constitution believed that the President should represent the nation as a whole in unity. This is the purpose of the Electoral College. This body of electors was intended to balance the need for national unity while protecting the sovereignty of the state governments. Unfortunately, the Electoral College is increasingly under attack by misguided Americans who fail to understand that in our Constitution the state governments have a vital role in our government. I highly recommend this book by Gary and Carolyn Alder. It is filled with valuable information concerning the proper role of the Electoral College, the best kept secret in American politics today."

—**David W. New**, Attorney at Law - author of:
*The Constitution for Beginners*
*The First Amendment and the Bill of Rights for Beginners*
*Religious Freedom in America for Beginners*

"A key to the United States of America sustaining liberty is education. We know constitutional illiteracy is one of the worst challenges facing us today. As we strive to find quality, informative, easy to understand teaching tools from time-to-time we find one extraordinary. *The Evolution and Destruction of the Original Electoral College* is such a tool. This little book takes the student on a journey of understanding from its opening to the conclusion urging a return to original design. We encourage everyone to read and share this book. Every election cycle you will be glad you did!"

—**Gary & Shirley Wood** – Co-founders of the Heritage Training Center www.heritagetrainingcenter.com

Re:
*The Evolution and Destruction of the Original Electoral College*
"Over 200 years ago, the Founders guaranteed a republican form of government. Instead, the Constitution has been amended and distorted to become what they feared most. Carolyn and Gary have effectively summarized how this happened."

—**Cherilyn Eagar**, Chairwoman,
National Eagle Forum Constitutional Studies

"Although the evolution of the Electoral College is very little spoken of today, the consequences of that evolution are the primary reason why we endure so much political intrigue and corruption in elections today. This booklet makes a compelling argument for a restoration of the principles that guided the Founders in their creation of the original Electoral College.

It was also a very refreshing read. I obtained an undergraduate degree in political science as well as a law degree and the Electoral College never came up. So, unfortunately, almost all of the concepts were new. As such, I believe the booklet should be a REQUIRED READING for all students graduating from college, and especially from law school."

**—Marcus Smith, J.D.**
University of North Carolina at Chapel Hill

"Gary and Carolyn Alder's *The Evolution and Destruction of the Original Electoral College* is a well-researched book that reviews the original concept behind the Electoral College. They looked into the original intent and came to the conclusion that if the Electoral College were implemented today in its original form, it would help do away with today's political party system that highlights moneyed special interests and corruption. Their conclusion is well founded. The book reflects solid research. I highly recommend it to anyone interested in solving the problems we face today with the present system."

**—Ken Bowers** – author of:
*Hiding in Plain Sight*
*Beneath the Tide*

"Gary and Carolyn Alder are right on target with their elucidation of the realms of freedom. The Alders have researched the Electoral College in a way that illuminates the intent of the founding fathers. I appreciate the Alders' love of freedom and our inspired Constitution. You can count on them!"

**—Jim Mackley** – *Sentinel News* Managing Editor,
Founder of the Freedom Coalition

"This is one of those booklets that I didn't want to set down—Even after I had read it several times. A real gem.

I majored in political science in college, with an emphasis on American political thought and the U.S. Constitution, and taught the Constitution to high school students. Furthermore I studied the Constitution and constitutional principles for over thirty-five years. So I thought I knew all about how the original Electoral College operated—Boy was I wrong.

I thought the Electoral College was primarily a candidate selection process. But Gary and Carolyn Alder explain how the Electoral College was a three step process involving nomination, candidate selection and a final vote. This process of nomination, candidate selection, and final vote is explored in detail.

Finally, the authors discuss the history of how the Electoral College was undermined, and how our modern political parties and our current flawed Presidential election process came into being.

I can't recommend this booklet highly enough. Simply marvelous."

   **—Steven Ray Montgomery** –
      Independent Constitutional Scholar and Researcher


"Thank you for all the well-researched evidence, inspired insight and wisdom packed into your book, *The Evolution and Destruction of the Original Electoral College.* Knowledge of the truth is the medicine my spirit needs to heal the devastating effects of historical deception and confusion.

The Electoral College has long been a subject of curiosity and interest, for I recognized that something wise and wonderful has become so battered and scarred that most Americans have tossed the whole concept in the 'has bin'.

Yet I had not knowledge enough to defend the principles behind its genius. Now I do; now I will."

   **—Susan Sorensen** – Former Salt Lake County Chair
      Constitution Party of Utah

"I finished your excellent book, *The Evolution and Destruction of the Original Electoral College.* You did a fantastic job. It's badly needed information. No question there is a strong movement to get rid of the Electoral College by the evildoers. I've spent nearly 21 years in the trenches full time. I like to say I've actually been in school the last two decades because I've learned more from researchers like you than in any classroom. I'll make sure I highlight it on my website. I want to keep my copy for reference in columns.

Thank you for all your hard work."

—**Devvy Kidd** – American Patriot Columnist for
    *News With Views* "Constitutionally Speaking"
    Founder and Director of POWER – The Project On Winning
    Economic Reform
    Author of: *Why a Bankrupt America* and *Blind Loyalty* (sold two
    million copies)


"The Alders' research on the history and evolution of the Electoral College is most impressive.  It is the best book I have ever read on the subject."

—**Frank Fluckiger** – National Chairman
    Constitution Party

# Table of Contents

# Foreword

By Michael A. Peroutka Esq.

Constitution Party Presidential Candidate, 2004
Co-Founder of *Institute on the Constitution*

Martin Luther once made the point that if his preaching and teaching were addressing everything but where, at the moment, the world and the Devil were attacking, he would be a failure: "If I profess with loudest voice and clearest exposition every portion of the truth of God except that little point which the world and the Devil are at that moment attacking, I am not confessing Christ, however boldly I may be professing Christ. Where the battle rages, there the loyalty of the soldier is proved, and to be steady on all the battlefield besides, is mere flight and disgrace if he flinches at that point."

And that is what is so important about the booklet in your hand by Gary and Carolyn Alder. It gives you ammunition to fight on the right side in an important political battle now raging–the fight to radically alter the form of government given us by our Founders (a Constitutional representative Republic) and change it to a pure democracy. In this battle, the Alders have not flinched.

In this well-researched booklet, the Alders make us aware of what the original Electoral College was. They believe it should be restored. They believe such a restoration would play a key role in reinstituting our original American Republic.

I strongly agree with the Alders that the original system our Founders gave us for electing Presidents/statesmen has, indeed, been "perverted, subverted, obscured, ignored and then discarded by the machinations of party politics." And one of the most insidious, pernicious attempted subversions

1

of our political system is to try to change it to a "pure democracy."

For example, a "New York Times" editorial headlined "Making Votes Count: Abolish The Electoral College" (8/29/2004) says, ignorantly, that the Electoral College is "a ridiculous setup, which thwarts the will of the majority"...[and] shocks people in other nations who have been taught to look upon the United States as the world's oldest democracy."

Well, now. I have no doubt people in other nations and, alas, most people in our own country have been taught that the United States is a "democracy." But, our Founders gave us a Constitutional representative Republic. They did not give us a "democracy!" In fact, our Founders hated and feared "democracy." They often referred to such a system as "mobocracy."

James Madison, "the Father of our Constitution," said, regarding "pure democracy" that "such democracies have ever been spectacles of turbulence and contention; have ever been found incompatible with personal security or the rights of property; and have in general been as short in their lives as they have been violent in their deaths. Theoretic politicians, who have patronized this species of government, have erroneously supposed that by reducing mankind to a perfect equality in their political rights, they would, at the same time, be perfectly equalized and assimilated in their possessions, their opinions, and their passions."

Alexis de Tocqueville said: "It cannot be denied that democratic institutions strongly tend to promote the feeling of envy in the human heart; not so much because they afford to everyone the means of rising to the same level with others as because those means perpetually disappoint the persons who employ them. Democratic institutions awaken and foster a passion for equality which they can never entirely

2

satisfy. This complete equality eludes the grasp of the people at the very moment when they think they have grasped it..."

In this excellent booklet, you will learn important details about:

— Direct vs. indirect elections.
— Democracy vs. Republic.
— The role of independent electors.
— How electoral votes are nominating votes.
— The principle of Federalism.
— How the process has been subverted by political parties.
— How the 12th Amendment institutionalized party usurpation.
— The empty shell we have today.

In their conclusion, the Alders say: "What seems like a small change in the beginning can have large consequences when allowed to go to fruition. The movement of only a few inches of a railroad track at a switch can cause a train to go a completely different direction. What seem like small and insignificant changes to the electoral system have us operating under a completely different paradigm than the Framers of the Constitution designed. ...In our opinion, having wise Electors nominate the most qualified presidential candidates is the way to go. The best answer by far is to return to the original design of the Framers as carefully outlined in Article II of the Constitution."

So true. Our country is, in so many ways, off-the-track and going in the wrong direction. We have ignored God for generations and are reaping that whirlwind (Psalm 9:17). Because we have ignored God, oaths mean nothing anymore to most of those who take them and that means our Constitution is not taken seriously.

Thank God, literally, for folks like the Alders. Thank you, Gary and Carolyn for this booklet.

# Introduction

When people ask us "How could this country create a system which would consistently produce high quality presidents?" Our answer is: "Focus on the quality of the candidates." Seek for statesmen rather than push a particular politician. Think long term. Concern yourself more with the candidate selection process rather than the final outcome of a particular election. The Framers of the Constitution created exactly that kind of system—the original Electoral College. This book reveals the secrets of that ingenious process—a system that has remained hidden (or rather ignored) for over two centuries.

Today the Electoral College bears only a superficial resemblance to what the Framers designed. Their original concept has been subverted, perverted, obscured, ignored and discarded. Today the Electors meet only to rubber-stamp what everybody already knows—who won the election.

Intelligent design vs. evolution regarding the creation of man has been an ongoing debate. We relate these same terms to the creation of our Constitution. Intelligent design requires much thought and consideration; evolution has no such restrictions. After the Framers intelligently designed the Electoral College System, the forces of evolution started their destructive processes.

First the original intent of the system was ignored. The Constitution was hastily amended to support the way the system was being manipulated. Making what appeared to be minor changes in the Constitution opened the door to further evolution, destroying the structure. Hence, the title: *The Evolution and Destruction of the Original Electoral College.*

The secret to understanding the original system is that the Electors were to nominate potential presidential candidates

5

not elect the President. They were to identify statesmen who had proven themselves through experience and service to their communities, states, and country. Imagine a system where wise individuals are seeking qualified people of integrity to nominate for president, where there is no personal aggrandizing, no campaigning, no campaign promises and no campaign financing.

This was the nature of the presidential selection process inherent in the original design of the Constitution. We believe that as the people of the United States become aware of the intelligent design, purpose and benefits of the original Electoral College System, they will rush to restore it.

As the constitutional specifications were ignored, misused, and modified, the resultant nature of the system became different. We designate these different natures of the presidential selection process as different versions of the system. We have organized the book into three main sections to contrast each of these versions.

In this book we will discuss the following topics:

a) The ingenious design of the original Electoral College System which we call the first version

b) How manipulation and cabal, culminating in the 12th Amendment, allowed political parties to subvert the original system creating a different version

c) How today's version of the Electoral College perverts the Electors' constitutionally assigned task

d) How the National Popular Vote compact intends to circumvent the remains of the Electoral College.

6

# Terms and Usage

In this book, we capitalize certain terms to designate a specific usage. The same terms in lower case indicate general usage; such as constitution, representative, elector, and electoral college. Representative (capitalized) means a member of the United States House of Representatives. Elector (capitalized) refers to an Elector for the President of the United States. Founders are those who laid the foundation for the nation. Framers are those who designed the Constitution.

The term *general government* was used by the Framers to indicate the national level of a federal government such as the United States under the Constitution. The term seemed less inflammatory to them than *national government* which could be considered a consolidated government.

The term *federal government* is commonly used today to refer to the national level of government. Unfortunately, the nature of our so called federal government is so far from federal that it resembles a dictatorship or an oligarchy more than a league of states. For this reason it would be counterproductive to use the terminology. While we extensively use the concepts of federalism as outlined in the Constitution in this book, we avoid using the term federal government rather than hazard miscommunication.

The term *national government* can validly be used to refer to either the level of government or to the nature of government. The term national government could therefore refer to a government which is federal in nature rather than consolidated. We use it in this book in the sense of the *level* of government. In *Federalist No. 39* James Madison superbly demonstrates the combination of these different federal and national *natures* in our original government as outlined in the Constitution.

The term *constitutional federalism* refers to the unique federal system created by the Constitution. Constitutional Federalism is a way of describing the complex constitutional representative republic that was designed by the Framers to share power between national and state governments. The term is used in contrast to the simple federation created by the Articles of Confederation but also in contrast to a consolidated national government or simple republic.

The term *electoral college system* in this book refers to the selection process for the President of the United States as outlined by the Constitution. One of the major components of the system is the college[1] or group of Electors known as the Electoral College. The system, however, is more important than any of its components or even more than the sum of all its components. It is often referred to by the name of its unique component, the Electoral College. When a more rigorous distinction is required we explicitly use the term Electoral College System.

The term *electoral college*[2] in this book primarily refers to the Electoral College System. As the context may require, we will sometimes refer to the Electoral College as all of the individual Electors. In discussions and debates during the Constitutional Convention, the Framers did not use the term

---

[1] see definition below

[2] Noah Webster, in his 1828 Dictionary, defines *electoral* and *college* as:
   **ELECTORAL** Pertaining to election or electors. The electoral college in Germany consisted of all the electors of the empire, being nine in number, six secular princes and three archbishops.

   **COLLEGE** In its primary sense, a collection or assembly. Hence,
   1. In a *general sense*, a collection, assemblage or society of men, invested with certain powers and rights, performing certain duties or engaged in some common employment or pursuit.
   2. In a *particular sense*, an assembly for a political or ecclesiastical purpose as the college of Electors or their deputies at the diet in Ratisbon. ...
   *American Dictionary of the English Language* (*Noah Webster 1828*)

electoral college but rather spoke of Electors as a group, even before they decided how to define the responsibilities of that group in the system they were designing.

The term *elector*[3] refers to an individual who is qualified and authorized to elect someone to office. Technically all voters are electors. (see *US Constitution* Article I Section 2 Clause 1) However, there is a special position in the United States designated to vote for a presidential candidate which nowadays is the common way we use the word *elector*—a presidential Elector. (see *US Constitution* Article II Section 1 Clause 2) Before popular elections were held in Europe and other areas of the world, various countries designated specific groups of government and church officials as delegates to elect other government officials. In those electoral college settings, electors differ from those we discuss in this book in that they are permanent in nature and usually are existing government officials.

The term *popular vote system* is simple majority rule. The term is used in this book as a contrast to Constitutional Federalism in general and specifically the Electoral College System for electing presidents. Popular vote generates political parties and is the basis for representative democracies, or simple republics which are consolidated national governments. It is the common system used by democracies around the world. Popular vote is the de facto system we currently use in the United States—not the system the Framers designed.

---

[3] An *elector* is defined by Noah Webster as follows:

**ELECTOR** One who elects, or one who has the right of choice; a person who has by law or constitution, the right of voting for an officer. In free governments, the people or such of them as possess certain qualifications of age, character and property, are the electors of their representatives &c, in parliament, assembly, or other legislative body. In the United States certain persons are appointed or chosen to be electors of the president or chief magistrate. (*Noah Webster 1828*)

# US Electoral College Different from Others

Although the original Electoral College precisely fits the dictionary definition of an electoral college, it was designed to be very different in practice than any electoral college that was known at the time. Other electoral colleges were designed to allow the aristocracy (in conjunction with the clergy) to select a new king in an elective monarchy. The electors therefore were chosen by their position and whoever held that position at the death of the old king was an elector to choose the new king regardless of personal merit or individual ability. Being an elector was just part of their job.

In contrast to the common model of electors and electoral colleges, presidential Electors in the United States are only appointed for a temporary assignment. These special delegates were not to be part of government. The Constitution expressly forbids Senators, Representatives, government officials or employees (a "person holding an office of trust or profit under the United States") from holding the office of an Elector. The spirit of these explicit instructions would also prohibit any individual under the influence of the general government from being an Elector. We explain the importance of this as we detail the particulars of the original Electoral College.

One other difference should be noted here. In other electoral colleges, the whole election process was in the hands of the electors. In the model designed by the Framers, only the nomination function of the election was turned over to the Electors—who were not part of government. Various government bodies were to handle the rest of the election process.

# Version 1 – INTELLIGENT DESIGN

## The Original Electoral College

Once one fully understands the Electoral College design as described in the original Constitution, he can readily see the evolution and deterioration brought about by political party influence and control that led to the passage of the 12th Amendment. From that point, examination of the further deterioration that has continued to obfuscate and confound the principles of this amazing system, leads one to recognize how the system evolved to the empty shell we have today. On the other hand, those who fail to understand in detail the characteristics of the original design will lack the baseline to adequately compare the modifications that were made to the original intent of the Framers as specified in the Constitution.

The mode of selecting a chief executive was analyzed and discussed throughout the entire Convention. The pros and cons of each proposal were extensively debated. It took until the last days of the Convention before they finally agreed upon the intricate design of the Electoral College System.[4]

---

[4] The Virginia Resolutions (read by Edmund Randolph on May 29, 1787), which served as a starting point for the new Constitution called for the executive to be chosen by the National Legislature. As early as June 2nd, the use of Electors in an indirect election of the president was considered as a way to keep from giving too much power to the general government in the selection of the president. James Wilson proposed having the people divided into districts and selecting Electors who would then elect a president. Elbridge Gerry: "seemed to prefer the taking of the suffrages of the States instead of Electors, or letting the Legislatures nominate and the Electors appoint." (*United States – Formation of the Union* p. 137)

The role of the Electors and the role of a branch of government (usually the Senate), was thus discussed off and on for the remainder of the Convention. The participation of the Senate was considered too aristocratic; a direct election too democratic; and the use of the House of Representatives or even both Houses of Congress too favorable to the large states at the expense of the small states.

*(footnote continues on next page)*

11

# Direct Election vs. Indirect Election

Let us first examine the concepts of direct and indirect election. In all republican governments except pure democracies (where all people vote directly on all issues), power is delegated (entrusted) to individuals to act in behalf of others. These individuals are known as delegates. To represent the interest of an individual, delegates are optional; to represent the interest of a group, they are indispensable. We intuitively understand this concept for delegates who will legislate (law makers). It is not as clear (or acceptable) when we consider delegates (electors) who vote in indirect elections.

Under the Articles of Confederation the interests of the people were only represented indirectly; the state legislatures chose the delegates to represent the interest of the States. The Framers of the Constitution wanted to retain this indirect representation, but wanted to also add direct representation. For this reason they designed one branch of the new government, the House of Representatives, to represent the interest of the people.[5] As individuals we represent our own

---

The decision to use the House voting by states rather than the Senate was not made until Sept. 6th. James Madison's notes of the Constitutional Convention read:

> Mr. WILLIAMSON suggested as better than an eventual choice by the Senate, that this choice should be made by the Legislature, voting by States and not per capita.
> Mr. SHERMAN suggested the House of Reps as preferable to the Legislature, and moved, accordingly, "To strike out the words 'The Senate shall immediately choose &c.' and insert 'The House of Representatives shall immediately choose by ballot one of them for President, the members from each State having one vote.'" (*United States – Formation of the Union* p. 678)

[5] Madison's Notes from the Constitutional Convention for May 31st 1787:
> Mr. MASON, argued strongly for an election of the larger branch by the people. It was to be the grand depository of the democratic principle of the Govtt. It was, so to speak, to be our House of Commons—It ought to know & sympathise with every part of the community; and ought therefore to be taken not only from different parts of the whole republic, but also from different districts of the

interest by personally voting for members of the House of Representatives.   That is the only interest that we are competent (inherently qualified) to represent.   That interest, unfortunately, is often manipulated.   In the Constitutional Convention, Elbridge Gerry from Massachusetts, expressed his opposition to what he termed "the excess of democracy" in this way:

> The evils we experience flow from the excess of democracy.  The people do not want [lack] virtue, but are the dupes of pretended patriots. In Mass[achusetts] it had been fully confirmed by experience that they are daily misled into the most baneful measures and opinions by the false reports circulated by designing men, and which no one on the spot can refute. (*United States – Formation of the Union* p. 125)

The protection against the evils of democracy that Mr. Gerry identified was that the positions in the other branches of government would be filled using indirect elections.  The *only* branch of the national government the people would vote for directly was the House of Representatives.

---

larger members of it, which had in several instances particularly in Virga., different interests and views arising from difference of produce, of habits &c &c. He admitted that we had been too democratic but was afraid we sd. incautiously run into the opposite extreme. We ought to attend to the rights of every class of the people. He had often wondered at the indifference of the superior classes of society to this dictate of humanity & policy; considering that however affluent their circumstances, or elevated their situations, might be, the course of a few years, not only might but certainly would, distribute their posterity throughout the lowest classes of Society. Every selfish motive therefore, every family attachment, ought to recommend such a system of policy as would provide no less carefully for the rights and happiness of the lowest than of the highest orders of Citizens. (*United States – Formation of the Union* p. 125-126)

The House of Representatives was to be balanced[6] by the Senate representing the interest of the state governments. Senators were to be appointed by the state legislatures. Presidents and judges were not to be directly elected by the people either. John Jay in *Federalist No. 64* explained the wisdom of the Convention in the superior method of electing both the President and the Senators by select bodies of delegates (electors) who would "in general be composed of the most enlightened and respectable citizens" in an indirect form of election.[7] The Framers intelligently designed the United States to be a complex constitutional representative republic

---

[6] Uriah Tracy, in the Senate debates on the 12th Amendment points out the following:

> The Constitution is nicely balanced, with the federative and popular principles; the Senate are the guardians of the former, and the House of Representatives of the latter; and any attempts to destroy this balance, under whatever specious names or pretenses they may be presented, should be watched with a jealous eye. (*The Founders' Constitution* vol. 5 p. 464)

[7] John Jay says:

> The power of making treaties is an important one, especially as it relates to war, peace, and commerce; and it should not be delegated but in such a mode, and with such precautions, as will afford the highest security that it will be exercised by men the best qualified for the purpose, and in the manner most conducive to the public good. The convention appears to have been attentive to both these points; they have directed the President to be chosen by select bodies of electors to be deputed by the people for that express purpose; and they have committed the appointment of senators to the State legislatures. This mode has, in such cases, vastly the advantage of [over] elections by the people in their collective capacity where the activity of party zeal, taking advantage of the supineness, the ignorance, and the hopes and fears of the unwary and interested, often places men in office by the votes of a small proportion of the electors.

> As the select assemblies for choosing the President, as well as the State legislatures who appoint the senators, will in general be composed of the most enlightened and respectable citizens, there is reason to presume that their attention and their votes will be directed to those men only who have become the most distinguished by their abilities and virtue, and in whom the people perceive just grounds for confidence. (*Federalist No. 64*)

***not*** a democracy.[8]  Today, we do not consider the concept of protecting separate and sometimes conflicting interests.[9]

The Framers developed a method to select the best presidents possible.  Now democracy (direct elections or popular vote) is assumed to be the only "fair" way to elect presidents as well as members of both branches of the national legislature.  A brief look at the caliber of candidates and the nature of the campaign rhetoric and tactics the current methods have produced at all levels should send us searching for a better method.  In our opinion, the original Constitution had the answers.  This book focuses on presidential elections.

## The Phases of Any Election Process

Let us next outline the three phases of any election process.  They can be described as:

1. Nomination—the ***possibilities***
2. Candidate Selection—the ***probabilities***
3. Final Vote—the ultimate selection—the ***pick***

Each of these phases pertains to a separate function that can be performed using one of the following election methodologies:

a) Direct election by the whole electorate (all voters) in a democracy
b) Indirect election by delegates in a representative republic
c) Indirect election for one phase and direct election for another phase
d) Indirect election by separate sets of delegates (electors) representing different interests for each phase.

---

[8] Key #12 (see "15 Key Principles" page 106) Explanation (www.freedomformula.us)

[9] Key #10 (see "15 Key Principles" page 106) Explanation (www.freedomformula.us)

The Framers designed a complex representative republic implementing all of these methods. They chose this last method (indirect election by separate sets of delegates) to select the President and Vice-President of the United States.[10]

# The Phases of the Electoral College System

Let us describe the purpose and function of the electoral system outlined in the Constitution in terms of these three phases. The original design can be summarized as follows:

## Nomination

1.  Each state was to designate a certain number of wise men, titled Electors, to nominate the best possible candidates for president.

## Candidate Selection

2.  Candidate selection was accomplished by counting the nominations; the five highest were the field of candidates. If a majority of the Electors nominated a particular individual, he would be named President, bypassing the deciding vote of the House of Representatives.

## Final Vote

3.  The House of Representatives would choose the President from among up to five individuals who

---

[10] In *Federalist No. 39*, James Madison explains:

> The executive power will be derived from a very compound source. The immediate election [Phase 1] of the President is to be made by the States in their political characters. The votes allotted to them are in a compound ratio, which considers them partly as distinct and coequal societies, partly as unequal members of the same society. The eventual election, [Phase 3] again, is to be made by that branch of the legislature which consists of the national representatives; but in this particular act they are to be thrown into the form of individual delegations, from so many distinct and coequal bodies politic. From this aspect of the government it appears to be of a mixed character, presenting at least as many *federal* as *national* features.

received the highest number of nominations by the Electors with each state casting one vote.[11]

A detailed explanation of the original Electoral College System will be done in terms of each of these separate phases. Please try to block out perceptions of how the system currently works. The current system will be described later in contrast to the original intent of the Framers. We first must understand the original design so that it can serve as our baseline.

## Phase 1 – Nomination

Each state was to designate a certain number of wise men, titled Electors, to nominate the best candidates for president.

Article II Section 1 of the Constitution explains the process as follows:

> *Each state shall appoint, in such manner as the Legislature thereof may direct, a number of Electors, equal to the whole number of Senators and Representatives to which the State may be entitled in the Congress: but no Senator or Representative, or person holding an office of trust or profit under the United States, shall be appointed an Elector.* (Article II Section 1 Clause 2)

### Each State Shall Appoint

*Each state shall appoint, in such manner as the Legislature thereof may direct* specifies that the method of appointing the presidential Electors was entirely left up to the discretion of the legislature of each state. Congress was not to regulate, control, or influence the appointment of presidential Electors. This power was the prerogative of the states. The

---

[11] See footnote 4 concerning the development of the mode for final vote.

appointments could be made directly by the legislature of each state; or each legislature could designate how the people of their state could participate in appointing the Electors. By recognizing and deferring to the competence of the states, the principle of Constitutional Federalism was maintained.

### Federalism in Practice

After nine states had ratified the Constitution, Congress (still under the authority of the Articles of Confederation) made provisions for the startup of the new government. On September 13, 1788, Congress adopted an election ordinance[12] that set the dates for the selection of presidential Electors and the date they would meet in their separate states to perform their duty.[13]

In exercising their prerogatives to appoint presidential Electors, the several states devised various combinations of legislative appointment and election by the people. Each state designed its own method. A few examples of how the states chose their Electors in 1789 follow.[14] In 1789 the Electors were to be appointed on January 7th (first Wednesday) and the Electors were to meet in their respective states on February 4th (first Wednesday).

MASSACHUSETTS:
On December 18, 1788, the people in each of the eight congressional districts "elected" (or essentially nominated) two Elector-candidates. On January 7, 1789, the state legislature (called the General Court) appointed one of the two Elector-candidates for each district. The General Court also appointed the commonwealth's two remaining (at-large) presidential Electors.

---

[12] *Documentary History of the First Federal Elections* vol. 1 p. ix

[13] *US Constitution* Article II Section 1 Clause 4

[14] Examples of methods mentioned by Richard E. Berg-Andersson (www.thegreenpapers.com/Hx/ByWhomElectorsWereAppointed.phtml) - accessed 10/10/2010

NEW JERSEY:
On January 7, 1789, the Governor and Privy Council[15] appointed the seven presidential Electors allotted to the state.

NEW HAMPSHIRE:
On November 5, 1788, the legislature met to elect their U.S. Senators and draft the election law regarding their three U.S. Representatives and their five presidential Electors. Monday December 15 was designated election day. Elections were at large rather than by district. The Elector-candidates failed to gain one-tenth of the popular vote,[16] so on January 7, 1789, the legislature (General Court) appointed the Electors from the top ten candidates.

NEW YORK:
Because of a dispute between the two chambers of the state legislature, New York did not settle on a method for the legislature to appoint their Electors. They proposed various compromises—such as each house appointing half of the Electors. The legislature was trying to arrive at a common method for appointing both their Electors and their U.S. Senators. They could not agree. It was not until July 1789 (long after the Electors had cast their votes) that New York appointed their state's first Senators. (Ironically, the seat of the new United States government was in New York City.)

As the state legislatures experimented with the appointment process in subsequent elections, they modified their procedures. In 1792 there were 15 states. The legislatures of

---

[15] Gordon DenBoer explains:
The election law authorized the "Governor and Council" to appoint presidential Electors. The state constitution of 1776 provided that the governor could convene any three or more members of the Legislative Council as a Privy Council at any time. It was thus in their capacity as privy councillors that eleven of the thirteen members of the Legislative Council met with the governor on 7 January 1789 to choose presidential Electors. (*Documentary History of the First Federal Elections* vol. 3 p.29)

[16] *Documentary History of the First Federal Elections* vol. 1 p. 770

9 states appointed the Electors. In 1796 there were 16 states. The legislatures of 9 states appointed the Electors that year also.[17] However, by 1836 all of the then 24 states, except South Carolina, had evolved to "appointment by the people" as the method. "Appointment by the people" did not mean all the people. The elective franchise was restricted to those who qualified. Each state determined its own voter qualifications.[18]

## A Number of Electors

Each state was to appoint *a number of Electors equal to the whole number of Senators and Representatives*. The number of Representatives is proportional to the population of the state and two Senators is a constant allocated to each state. Thus the number is equal to the total congressional representation for each state. Notice that only the number of presidential Electors for each state is determined by following these instructions. The actual Senators and Representatives in office are precluded from being Electors.

It has been said that the formula for determining the number of Electors is weighted to favor the small (less populous) states. We consider it to slightly reduce the advantage the large (more populous) states have. It must be remembered that the Framers were moving from a paradigm of equal representation of all states under the Articles of Confederation to a bi-cameral congress with one house represented by population (a new idea at that time) and the other house retaining the equal representation concept of the former system. Using this number does not dilute the influence of large states very much. It does increase the percentage of each small state's tiny influence. The states with one Representative benefit most.

---

[17] *The Founders' Constitution* vol. 3 pp. 552-553

[18] Those who qualified to elect the officials of the most numerous Branch of the State Legislature were constitutionally competent (qualified) to elect Representatives for the U.S. House of Representatives. (see *US Constitution* Article I Section 2 Clause 1)

## Numerical Analysis

We will compare the number of Electors that are allocated to several of the states using the weighted figures with the number of Electors that would have been allocated if the Framers had used only the number of Representatives. The figures show the percentage of the whole number of Electors for each state's weighted and non-weighted number. The District of Columbia has no Representatives or Senators; therefore its Electors (see Amendment 23) are not included in these calculations.

### Relative Electoral Weights of States[19]

| State | Electors House + 2 | Percent of 535 | Electors House Only | Percent of 435 |
|---|---|---|---|---|
| California | 55 | 10.28% | 53 | 12.18% |
| Texas | 38 | 7.10% | 36 | 8.28% |
| New York | 29 | 5.42% | 27 | 6.21% |
| Illinois | 20 | 3.74% | 18 | 4.14% |
| New Jersey | 14 | 2.62% | 12 | 2.76% |
| Tennessee | 11 | 2.06% | 9 | 2.07% |
| Maryland | 10 | 1.87% | 8 | 1.84% |
| Utah | 6 | 1.12% | 4 | 0.92% |
| Wyoming | 3 | 0.56% | 1 | 0.23% |

Notice that states with nine Representatives have the same percentage using either method.

### Electors an Independent Body

Let us now examine the nature of those Electors. If the spirit of the words *no Senator or Representative, or person holding an office of trust or profit* were to be followed, any Elector that was beholden to any of the incumbents would be precluded as well. What good would it do to preclude the

---

[19] 2010 Census figures.

direct participation of the current members of government if, in their place, proxies were sent who would vote the will of the ones precluded? The Electors' votes were to be their own. The Framers wanted to protect against a system with any kind of political payoff. To accomplish this, the Electors were set up as a temporary body not associated with government. The system was set up so that those who nominated could not elect and those that were to elect could not nominate.

## Electoral Votes are Nominating Votes

The common understanding of the word *vote* implies a final election. In other electoral colleges, the vote of the Electors is the final determination. The initial naming (or nomination) of candidates is also a form of voting or selecting. We will demonstrate that in the American Electoral College System, the duty of each Elector was to nominate (and only nominate) possible presidential candidates. In the absence of an exceptional circumstance, the House of Representatives would choose the President.[20]

For this discussion we use examples with current numbers but simulate the function of the original system. The essence of the argument for the weighted model shown in the chart on page 21 is: Adding two Electors for each state regardless of population would add four votes per state equally, because each Elector would nominate two persons for president.

With 55 Electors rather than 53, California could have submitted 110 votes instead of 106 votes. With six Electors rather than four, Utah could have submitted 12 votes rather

---

[20] The concept of having one body nominate a group of candidates from which another body will make a final selection is consistent with Resolution number 5 of the Virginia Plan:

> The Committee proceeded to Resolution 5. "that the second, [or senatorial] branch of the National Legislature ought to be chosen by the first branch out of persons nominated by the State Legislatures." (Madison's Notes – Constitutional Convention - May 31st *United States – Formation of the Union* p. 127)

than eight votes. With three Electors rather than one, Wyoming could have submitted six votes instead of two votes. The additional votes would not add an equal percentage, but *no state would lose votes*. In a final election where the object is to eliminate all but one candidate this seems counterintuitive. Recognizing this as a nomination function however, it would not only be logical and reasonable, but it would be very desirable to collect additional possibilities for consideration.

Let us examine Article II Section 1 Clause 3 to analyze the details of that process.

> *The Electors shall meet in their respective states, and vote by ballot for two persons, of whom one at least shall not be an inhabitant of the same state with themselves. And they shall make a list of all the persons voted for, and of the number of votes for each; which list they shall sign and certify, and transmit sealed to the Seat of the Government of the United States, directed to the President of the Senate.*
> (Article II Section 1 Clause 3)

### Meet in Their Respective States

The Electors' function was to nominate. *The Electors shall meet in their respective states*—one meeting of the Electors in their own state. It is significant to note that there was to be no connection with the Electors of other states, no campaigning, no trading of votes for future influence, or "supporting your program if you support mine." They were to give it their best shot first—because that was the only shot they had.

In fact, the Electors met in their separate states on the same day to avoid the chance of collaborating with the Electors from other states during this process. The Electors in each state were able to freely discuss among themselves which individuals were most qualified to be president. They were

23

not, however, forced to conform to the nominations of other Electors from their state. Each Elector's independent decision of which two individuals to nominate was preserved and respected.

The Electors do not represent the interest of their state alone but rather the interest of the nation as a whole. Realizing that the purpose of the Electoral College is only to nominate potential presidential candidates, it is evident that normally another body will make the final decision. That body is the House of Representatives. Even though the Electors meet by state, no individual state has enough influence to force any particular outcome on a national basis.

## Vote by Ballot for Two Persons

Each Elector was to *vote by ballot for two persons*. Do we have any evidence that there was a pre-printed ballot? Of course not. That would pre-suppose a separate nominating process. Each Elector wrote down two names. In other words they named or nominated two candidates for president. Every time we write-in a candidate we nominate that candidate. The existence of pre-printed ballots would be proof that there was a separate nominating process. If a separate nominating process existed and that process were not described in detail in the Constitution, that fact alone would be evidence of a serious design flaw in the Constitution.

If the Electors as a body were to make the final decision for president, the original Constitution would have required each Elector to make a final decision—that is to vote for only one candidate. The very fact that each Elector was to submit two equal choices, is strong evidence that the Electors' duty was to nominate candidates for a separate and subsequent final vote. This evidence therefore stands in direct opposition to the concept that the Electors were to make the final decision. Electoral votes were to be nominating votes, not deciding votes.

We have found that mentioning the word *nominate* seems to excite opposition and resistance. Nevertheless, when we examine more closely the process we see that originally it was intended to be a nomination. In the Constitutional Convention on September 5, 1787, as the mode of election of the President was getting close to the final design, Roger Sherman from Connecticut, and Rufus King from Massachusetts, made statements showing that the Electors were to nominate presidential candidates.

According to James Madison's notes on Sept. 5, Mr. Sherman used the word *nomination* to show that the Senate (changed to the House in the final design)[21] would choose from the candidates nominated by the Electors:

> Mr. SHERMAN reminded the opponents of the new mode proposed that if the small states had the advantage in the Senate's deciding among the five highest candidates, the large States would have in fact the nomination of these candidates (*United States – Formation of the Union* p. 670)

Although Mr. King did not use the word *nomination*, he contrasts the concept of nomination with final or deciding vote:

> Mr. KING observed that the influence of the Small States in the Senate[22] was somewhat balanced by the influence of the Large States in bringing forward the candidates; (*United States – Formation of the Union* p. 671)

---

[21] On Sept. 6, according to Madison's notes, the final vote was changed from the Senate to the House. Roger Sherman moved:
> To strike out the words "The Senate shall immediately choose &c." and insert "The House of Representatives shall immediately choose by ballot one of them for President, the members from each State having one vote." (*United States – Formation of the Union* p. 678)

[22] (see footnote 21)

James Madison made a similar contrast on the previous day, although at that time he was not in favor of the proposal.[23]

Gouverneur Morris, delegate from Pennsylvania, also uses the word **nominated** in describing the Electors' role in nominating candidates for the Senate[24] to choose from.  Mr. Morris said:

> ...by this they were limited to five candidates previously nominated to them, with a probability of being barred altogether by the successful ballot of the Electors. (*United States – Formation of the Union* p. 674)

This fact is further substantiated by the statements of Connecticut Senator Uriah Tracy made during the Senate debate on the 12th Amendment on Dec. 1, 1803.  Mr. Tracy, when describing the original intent of the Constitution, uses **nominate** when he said:

> Nothing can be more obvious, than the intention of the plan adopted by our Constitution for choosing a President.  The Electors are to nominate two persons, of whom they cannot know which will be president; this circumstance not only induces them to select both from the best men; but gives a direct advantage into the hands of the small states even in the electoral choice. (*The Founders' Constitution* vol. 5 p. 464)

---

[23] On Sept 4, James Madison said:

Mr. MADISON was apprehensive that by requiring both the President & vice President to be chosen out of the five highest candidates, the attention of the electors would be turned too much to making candidates instead of giving their votes in order to a definitive choice.  Should this turn be given to the business, the election would, in fact be consigned to the Senate altogether. It would have the effect at the same time, he observed, of giving the nomination of the candidates to the largest States. (*United States – Formation of the Union* p. 662)

[24] The body to represent the states was changed from the Senate to the House on the same day but after Gouverneur Morris's statement.
(see footnote 21 page 25)

Later in the same speech Mr. Tracy clarifies the details of the process when he says: "As the Constitution stands each Elector is to write the names of two persons on a piece of paper called a ballot." (*The Founders' Constitution* vol. 5 p. 467)

## One Not from Their Own State

To protect against the anticipated bias that the Electors would have in favor of only choosing men from their own state, the Constitution specified that *one at least shall not be an inhabitant of the same state with themselves*. This restriction would force each Elector to look outside of his own state for at least one nominee. Requiring each Elector to vote for at least one individual from a state other than his own, also prevented any particular state from dominating the process. There was no requirement that all votes from a state go to the same individuals; that would be inconsistent with the concept of nomination. Even though each Elector was required to nominate at least one individual from a state other than his own, the expectation was that the Electors of a state would not know or care how the Electors of another state were voting. In this way, the "will" of their state in this matter was also preserved.

## They Shall Make a List

Each state was to *make a list of all the persons voted for, and of the number of votes for each which list they shall sign and certify, and transmit sealed to the Seat of the Government of the United States, directed to the President of the Senate* for the candidate selection process (Phase 2) followed by the voting process (Phase 3). The Electors' job (Phase 1) was over.

# Hamilton Defends the System

In *Federalist No. 68* Alexander Hamilton explains and defends the Electoral College System. The entire text of *Federalist 68* is included with our comments interspersed. Brief comments are included [in brackets] within quoted segments. Clarifying and editorial comments of a more lengthy nature are separate paragraphs:

> March 12, 1788
> **To the People of the State of New York:**
>
> The mode of appointment of the chief magistrate of the United States is almost the only part of the system, of any consequence, which has escaped without severe censure, or which has received the slightest mark of approbation from its opponents. [Little else in the Constitution has escaped criticism and even received approval from those opposed to its ratification.] The most plausible of these, who has appeared in print, has even deigned [thought worthy] to admit that the election of the president is pretty well guarded. I venture somewhat further, and hesitate not to affirm, that if the manner of it be not perfect, it is at least excellent. [It sounds like Mr. Hamilton thinks it is a pretty good method.] It unites in an eminent degree all the advantages, the union of which was to be desired.

The debate in the Convention[25] concerning how to elect a president was one of the most difficult problems addressed by

---

[25] James Madison in a letter to Thomas Jefferson dated 24 Oct., 1787 lists various modes of selecting the president discussed in the Convention:

"The modes of appointment proposed were various, as by the people at large – by electors chosen by the people – by the Executives of the States – by the Congress, some preferring a joint ballot of the two Houses – some a separate concurrent ballot allowing to each a negative on the other house – some a nomination of several

the Framers. Although the decision was to use the Electoral College System to obtain candidates, the final design was not agreed upon until Sept. 6. (see footnote 21 page 8)

> It was desirable, that the sense of the people should operate in the choice of the person to whom so important a trust was to be confided. [This is not to be confused with a vote of the people after hearing the propaganda of political campaigns.] This end will be answered by committing the right of making it, not to any preestablished body, [such as the incumbents in government or a political faction or party] but to men chosen by the people for the special purpose, and at the particular conjuncture.[26]

> It was equally desirable, that the immediate election...[27]

Although Mr. Hamilton does not use the word "nomination", the phrase "immediate election" certainly shows that this is a preliminary selection rather than a final one. If the final choice were to be the sense intended, it would be called a final, ultimate, or eventual election.

> ...should be made by men most capable of analyzing the qualities adapted to the station, [analysts are required here not salesmen to excite the uninformed masses] and acting under circumstances favorable to

---

candidates by one House, out of whom a choice should be made by the other. Several other modifications were started. The expedient at length adopted seemed to give pretty general satisfaction to the members." (*The Founders' Constitution* vol. 1 p. 644)

[26] **CONJUNCTURE**
(def 2) An occasion; a critical time, proceeding from a union of circumstances. *Juncture* is used in a like sense... (*Noah Webster 1828*)

[27] The authors use ellipses (...) here to indicate a more lengthy interruption of a paragraph of *Federalist 68*—not that part of the text is missing from the quote.

deliberation, and to a judicious combination of all the reasons and inducements which were proper to govern their choice. A small number of persons, selected by their fellow-citizens from the general mass, [not part of or tied to government] will be most likely to possess the information and discernment requisite to such complicated investigation. [Wise men were to be chosen to select or nominate the best possible candidates.]

It was also peculiarly desirable, to afford as little opportunity as possible to tumult and disorder. [Such as campaigning, making false claims about one's own virtues, and telling of the real or imagined faults of an opponent.] This evil was not least to be dreaded in the election of a magistrate, who was to have so important an agency [responsibility] in the administration of the government, as the president of the United States. But the precautions which have been so happily concerted [working so well together] in the system under consideration, promise an effectual security against this mischief. The choice of *several*, to form an intermediate body of Electors, [between the people and the candidates] will be much less apt to convulse the community, with any extraordinary or violent movements than the choice of *one* who was himself to be the final object of the public wishes. [Someone tooting his own horn.] And as the Electors, chosen in each state, are to assemble and vote in the State, in which they are chosen, this detached and divided situation will expose them much less to heats and ferments, [arguments and campaigning] which might be communicated from them to the people, than if they were all to be convened at one time, in one place.

The Framers were opposed to demagoguery or rabble rousing. Rather than cater to the desires of individuals that might be seeking office for their own power and advantage, the Framers wanted the States to seek out wise individuals as Electors who were charged with the responsibility of finding worthy candidates. Although the Electors in each state were free to discuss their preferences, they were not to make one state's choices coordinate with those of any other state. This demonstrates that the primary concern was to get the best possible candidates. This is the nature of a nomination process rather than a final choice.

Alexander Hamilton continues to explain:

> Nothing was more to be desired, than that every practicable obstacle should be opposed to cabal,[28] intrigue[29] and corruption. These most deadly adversaries of republican government might naturally have been expected to make their approaches from more than one quarter, but chiefly from the desire in foreign powers to gain an improper ascendant[30] in our councils. How could they better gratify this, than by raising a creature of their own to the chief magistracy of the union? [Don't make a pitch to us, we will select candidates from those we already know and respect.] But the convention have guarded against all

---

[28] **CABAL**

1. A number of persons united in some close design; usually to promote their private views in church or state by intrigue. A junto. It is sometimes synonymous with faction, but a cabal usually consists of fewer men than a party, and the word generally implies close union and secret intrigues. This name was given to the ministry of Charles II., Clifford, Ashley, Buckingham, Arlington, and Lauderdale, the initials of whose names compose the word.

2. Intrigue; secret artifices of a few men united in a close design. (*Noah Webster 1828*)

[29] **INTRIGUE**

1. A plot or scheme of a complicated nature intended to effect some purpose by secret artifices... (*Noah Webster 1828*)

[30] **ASCENDANT**

1. Superiority or commanding influence; as, one man has the *ascendant* over another. (*Noah Webster 1828*)

danger of this sort, with the most provident and judicious attention. They have not made the appointment of the president to depend on any preexisting bodies of men [including current office holders and political parties] who might be tampered with beforehand to prostitute their votes; [for personal gain or agenda] but they have referred it in the first instance to an immediate[31] act of the people of America, to be exerted in the choice of persons for the temporary and sole purpose of making the appointment. [The Electors were to have no connection with the outcome of the choices they would make.] And they have excluded from eligibility to this trust, all those who from situation might be suspected of too great devotion to the president in office. No senator, representative, or other person holding a place of trust or profit under the United States, can be of the numbers of the Electors. [This is designed to reduce the bias toward the incumbent to favor a more objective approach.] Thus, without corrupting the body of the people, the immediate agents in the election will at least enter upon the task, free from any sinister byass [sic]. Their transient [temporary] existence, and their detached situation, [each state meeting separately] already taken notice of, afford a satisfactory prospect of their continuing so, to the conclusion of it. The business of corruption, when it is to embrace so considerable a number of men, requires time, as well as means. [It would take time and money to corrupt the process.] Nor would it be found easy suddenly to embark them, dispersed as they would be over thirteen states, in any

---

[31] It appears here that Alexander Hamilton is talking about the people of America directly voting for the presidential Electors. Although that is the way it ended up, we remind the reader that Article II Section 1 Clause 2 of the Constitution specifies that the state legislatures are to determine the mode of appointment; so at the time that the Federalist Papers were being written, this would only be an assumption on the part of Mr. Hamilton.

combinations, founded upon motives, which though they could not properly be denominated corrupt, might yet be of a nature to mislead them from their duty. [Remove even the temptation of corruption.]

Another and no less important desideratum [Latin - that which is desired] was, that the Executive should be independent for his continuance in office on all, but the people themselves. [He was not to be beholden to any special interests.] He might otherwise be tempted to sacrifice his duty to his complaisance[32] for those whose favor was necessary to the duration of his official consequence. [Those who could keep him in office.]

This advantage will also be secured, by making his re-election to depend on a special body of representatives, deputed by the society for the single purpose of making the important choice. [Rather than depending upon party or other elected officials.]

All these advantages will be happily combined in the plan devised by the convention; which is, that the people of each state shall choose a number of persons as Electors, equal to the number of senators and representatives of such state in the national[33] government, who shall assemble within the state, and vote for some fit person as president. ...

The whole design and purpose of the Electoral College was to nominate the individuals (plural) most fit for the office of President. The Electors were only to be involved in the first phase of the process. Presidential candidate nomination was

---

[32] **COMPLAISANCE**
   (def 2) Condescension; obliging compliance with the wishes or humors of others... (*Noah Webster 1828*)

[33] We believe Alexander Hamilton is referring to the level of government.

the prerogative of the Electors. They had no right, duty, or responsibility to be involved in the other two phases of the process. If, as we claim, the Electors were not given the names of nominees from some self-promoting candidate or his campaign staff, then what criteria would each Elector have to judge the best nominees? The answer would have to be their knowledge of the performance of those individuals in previous service to their cities, states, and country.

One of the most effective means of preventing the Electors from campaigning for a particular presidential candidate was for each of them to nominate two individuals. An Elector would have no way of knowing which (or if either) would be candidates to be voted on by a separate body of men. Designating which of his nominees was to be only a vice-presidential choice was not an Elector's prerogative. For most people who look at candidates "running for office" this concept is nearly impossible to understand. The Framers felt that the office should seek for the man not the man seek for the office. Unless the reader is willing to push the concept of a candidate "running for office" out of his mind, the words of Article II of the Constitution won't make much sense.

After the Electors completed their task of nomination, the results for their state were tallied and those results sent to the seat of government. The job assigned to the Electors was over. Their term of office (one meeting) was complete and they returned to private life. Weeks later, those results would be used in Phase 2 (candidate selection).

To give the reader a feel for the possibilities, let us provide some statistical details. In the first presidential election, 69 Electors from 10 states participated. Each Elector nominated 2 individuals. There could have been as few as 2 nominees if all the Electors nominated the same individuals. There could have been as many as 138 nominees if none of the Electors nominated the same individuals. In today's numbers with 538 Electors (including the District of Columbia) the numbers could be between 2 and 1076. For the candidate selection process to work, the system presupposes multiple nominations for outstanding individuals. When the Electors consider previous public service experience and performance as the criteria for selection, it is logical that the number of nominees will be much lower than the maximum possible.

## Phase 2 - Candidate Selection

Candidate selection was accomplished by counting the nominations; the five highest were the field of candidates. If a majority of the Electors nominated a particular individual, he would be named President, bypassing the deciding vote of the House of Representatives.

### Open the Certificates

In the Constitution it is described as follows:

*The President of the Senate shall, in the Presence of the Senate and House of Representatives, open all the Certificates, and the Votes shall then be counted.* (Article II Section 1 Clause 3)

At the designated time, the sealed, certified lists from each state were to be opened and tallied in the presence of the Senate and House as witnesses—narrowing the field to five candidates. *...from the five highest on the List the said House shall in like Manner choose the President.* (Article II Section 1 Clause 3) This method of determining candidates is not a result of debate or discussion. Five individuals nominated by the most Electors were to be presented to the House of Representatives for their final selection.

In a system free from intrigue and cabal, it seems rather intuitive that the House would almost always choose[34] the

---

[34] George Mason seems to agree with our analysis on this issue. He was not,

president from these five candidates. When the sealed electoral votes are opened and counted there is a possibility that one outstanding individual will have been recognized by a majority of the Electors. The Constitution provides a shortcut:

## The Shortcut

In order to adequately explain what we call the shortcut, we must focus on the objective of the whole Electoral College System which is to find the best possible presidential candidates. A consensus of independent Electors as the nominating votes are counted would indicate an extraordinary individual has been identified.

The Constitution describes this consensus:

> ***The Person having the greatest Number of Votes shall be the President, if such Number be a Majority of the whole number of Electors appointed***; (Article II Section 1 Clause 3)

If the individual with the highest number of electoral votes was nominated by a majority of the Electors, the final vote of the House of Representatives is bypassed. If more than one individual has that distinction, the final vote goes to the House anyway.

---

however, in favor of the Senate making the final choice. Madison, in his Convention notes on Sept. 4, records the following:

> Col: MASON confessed that the plan of the Committee had removed some capital objections, particularly the danger of cabal and corruption. It was liable however to this strong objection, that nineteen times in twenty the President would be chosen by the Senate, an improper body for the purpose. (*United States – Formation of the Union* p. 663)

When the final election was changed from the Senate to the House of Representatives Mr. Madison records: "Col: MASON liked the latter mode best as lessening the aristocratic influence of the Senate." (*United States – Formation of the Union* p. 678)

The Constitution continues:

> *and if there be more than one who have such Majority, and have an equal Number of Votes, then the House of Representatives shall immediately choose by Ballot one of them for President; and if no Person have a Majority, then from the five highest on the List the said House shall in like Manner choose the President.* (Article II Section 1 Clause 3)

The system was designed so that the Electors themselves would not have the means to force the shortcut by having the Electors meet in their respective states on the same day. The Framers also depended upon the independence of the Electors which means that the concurrence of electoral votes would be a matter of coincidence rather than design.

Technically up to three individuals could tie with votes from over half of the Electors because each Elector submits two names. Speaking in percentages, a president could be elected with a vote of just over 50% of the Electors. Since each Elector casts two votes, that would be just over 25% of the total electoral votes. Although we believe this would be very unlikely to happen, it is possible.[35] This also demonstrates that both persons named by an Elector have equal weight in the vote counting. There is no provision for a first and second

---

[35] Madison's Convention notes (Sept. 5) show that Gouverneur Morris substantiates our figures but concludes that the majority of Electors would nominate the same individual frequently:

> ...It is probable that a majority of votes will fall on the same man. As each elector is to give two votes, more than ¼ will give a majority. Besides as one vote is to be given to a man out of the State, and as this vote will not be thrown away, ½ the votes will fall on characters eminent & generally known. Again if the President shall have given satisfaction, the votes will turn on him of course, and a majority of them will reappoint him, without resort to the Senate: If he should be disliked, all disliking him, would take to unite their votes so as to ensure his being supplanted.

(*United States – Formation of the Union* p. 669)

choice.  Please keep this point in mind as we proceed to discuss the other versions of the electoral process.

In *Federalist No. 68* Alexander Hamilton describes this same concept, although with some inaccuracy (as a somewhat rigorous study of the above paragraphs shows).

> ...Their [independent] votes, thus given, are to be transmitted to the seat of the national government, and the person who may happen [incidentally not purposely] to have a majority of the whole number of votes will be the president. ...

A plurality[36] of electoral votes is not sufficient to bypass the election process by the House of Representatives; nomination by a majority of the Electors is required.  Unless one individual is obviously more qualified than anyone else, the Electors will submit many names.

Let us describe it another way.  If the individual with the highest number of nominating votes was nominated by over half of the Electors—in a situation where the Electors would not know the outcome from the Electors in other states, no final election is needed.  It is obvious that a person that outstanding should be president.

This was the case with our first President, George Washington.  Besides being the General who led in the fight for independence, he was so influential that there would not have been a Constitutional Convention had he not been there.  It is no surprise that George Washington was chosen as president of the Constitutional Convention.  When it came time for the Electors to nominate outstanding individuals as

---

[36] **PLURALITY**
> (def 3) In elections, a plurality of votes is when one candidate has more votes than any other, but less than half of the whole number of votes given. It is thus distinguished from a majority, which is more than half of the whole number. *(Noah Webster 1828)*

presidential candidates, he would be high on the list of patriots. In fact, George Washington was unanimously nominated. His name was one of the two names submitted by each Elector in 1789 and also in 1792.

After serving two terms as President, George Washington determined that he would not accept another nomination as president saying that two terms is long enough for any man to serve. He had his farewell address printed in the newspaper[37] so that everyone would know that he would retire at the end of his second term. This created a problem for future Electors because the most obvious choice was now unavailable. Even after making it clear that he would not accept the nomination, in 1796 two Electors voted for George Washington.

In the election of 1796, John Adams, who served as Vice-President to President George Washington, received the nominating vote of a majority of Electors. Thomas Jefferson received the next highest number of electoral votes and became Vice-President. There is some evidence that we were starting down the path to party rule in American politics by attempting to force or manipulate the shortcut, but we will address that later. Let us now discuss the election process in the House of Representatives.

## Phase 3 - Final Vote

The House of Representatives would choose the President from among up to five individuals who received the highest number of nominations by the Electors with each state casting one vote.

### The House of Representatives Shall Choose

Whether the House is choosing between five candidates, or resolving a tie in the highest number of electoral votes, the process is the same.

---

[37] Washington's farewell address was first published September 19, 1796 in Philadelphia's *American Daily Advertiser*.

The Constitution states:

> *...the said House shall in like manner choose the President. But in choosing the President, the votes shall be taken by States, the representation from each state having one vote*; (Article II Section 1 Clause 3)

We claim that without outside influence, independent Electors would usually nominate many qualified individuals from which five candidates would normally be sent to the House for a final vote. In addition to the usual field of five candidates, a very exceptional condition could create a field of two or three candidates. If a majority of the Electors happened to nominate the same two or three individuals with an equal number of votes, the House would decide between the tied candidates.

## Each State Has One Vote

When the election of the President goes to the House of Representatives, the members act as a delegation representing their states, similar to the delegations from each state in the Continental Congress under the Articles of Confederation. This same structure was also used during the Constitutional Convention. The phrase *in choosing the President, the votes shall be taken by States, the representation from each state having one vote* shows the desire to retain the federal nature of the Union.

The Representatives of the people, because they cast only one vote per state, act in the capacity of representing equally the will of the people of each state. If the vote were taken in the Senate (prior to the ratification of the 17th Amendment) the vote would represent the will of the government of each state. Another problem would occur if the deciding vote by state were taken in the Senate. Because each state has two Senators, the probability of a split vote is increased which would nullify the vote of that state.

Small states have as much say as large states. The equal vote by each state preserves the principle of federalism. This demonstrates that the office of President is not to be confused with a king of the people. He is President of the Union of States. A majority of the states is required to elect a President, not merely a plurality. This is a majority of the states, not a majority of the population, or a majority of the Representatives.

One caution: A state with an even number of Representatives, or Representatives who choose to abstain, could negate the vote of their state, making a majority of states more difficult to achieve. This system assumes that the "States' men" are statesmen choosing a statesman to watch over the best interest of their nation, rather than fighting over personal, regional or political biases.

## Vice-President Selection

Since the Vice-President would become President upon the death or removal from office of the President, that individual should also be one that had the same esteem and perceived virtue and capability as the President. He would therefore be chosen from the same pool of up to five candidates produced by counting the electoral votes.

The Constitution specifies:

> *In every Case, after the Choice of the President, the Person having the greatest Number of Votes of the Electors shall be the Vice President. But if there should remain two or more who have equal Votes, the Senate shall choose from them by Ballot the Vice President.* (Article II Section 1 Clause 3)

The Vice-President would always be the remaining presidential candidate with the most electoral votes after the

President was selected—the Senate would only choose if more than one had that number.

Our analysis indicates that strictly following the constitutional instructions and intent, the House would normally be involved in the selection of the President. The Senate would almost never choose the Vice-President.

## Original Design Summary

1.  The nomination process was accomplished by the Electoral College and amounted to a weighted vote. The reason for using the total congressional representation, Senators and Representatives, rather than only the number of Representatives, was to give smaller states more say in nominating possible presidential candidates, without disadvantaging larger states.

2.  The candidate selection was to take place as the nominations were opened and counted in a joint meeting of both houses of Congress. A field of up to 5 candidates was thereby created. An overwhelming nomination of a particular individual coming from the Electors (who were expected to be independent of outside influence) was taken as the will of the people and was not to be overridden (the shortcut). In other words if the President were selected by the Electors' nominations, it would be by coincidence rather than by strategy.

3.  Unless a majority of the total number of Electors nominated the same individual, as determined in the joint meeting, a field of up to five candidates would go to the House of Representatives where each state, regardless of population, would have an equal vote for the President.

When we were kids, our mothers taught us that in order to share a cookie or a candy bar with a friend, we would cut it in half; our friend would then choose his piece first. It is only fair. This is analogous to the situation with the electoral system. The Electors as independent representatives of the people, nominate the candidates; the House of Representatives decides which of those candidates becomes President. Each state casts one vote.

Now to return to Alexander Hamilton in *Federalist 68*:

> But as a majority of the votes might not always happen to centre on one man and as it might be unsafe to permit less than a majority to be conclusive, it is provided, that in such a contingency, the house of representatives shall select out of the candidates, who shall have the five highest number of votes, the man who in their opinion may be best qualified for the office.

It is apparent that the Framers were overly optimistic in expecting a consensus of the nominations coming from the Electoral College. Perhaps they thought that some outstanding individual like George Washington would become obvious to the Electors. In our opinion, there is no indication that the selection of a president by the House of Representatives was initially thought to be a big problem. Within a few years, however, this did become an issue.

> This process of election affords a moral certainty, that the office of president, will seldom[38] fall to the lot of any man, who is not in an eminent degree endowed with the requisite qualifications.

Alexander Hamilton indicates that this process of election (including the nominating role of the college of Electors) is what assures the high quality of presidential candidates. In our day, the words used by partisan candidates while

---

[38] Several quotes from Federalist 68 on the internet use the word *never*, including Yale University Avalon Project (http://avalon.law.yale.edu/18th_century/fed68.asp - accessed 3/11/2011)

campaigning under our current methods of election show that none of the candidates think of their opponents as endowed with superior qualifications.

Hamilton continues:

> Talents for low intrigue and the little arts of popularity may alone suffice to elevate a man to the first honors in a single state; but it will require other talents and a different kind of merit to establish him in the esteem and confidence of the whole union, or of so considerable a portion of it as would be necessary to make him a successful candidate for the distinguished office of president of the United States. It will not be too strong to say, that there will be a constant probability of seeing the station filled by characters pre-eminent for ability and virtue.

The method of selection of presidential Electors and presidential candidates is wholly to be credited with this prediction. A presupposition that wise Electors who know how to nominate individuals of character, experience, virtue, and integrity underlies the whole process. The wisdom and integrity of the Electors is essential. The independence of the Electors (that they are not "owned" by any group) is even more crucial. For the system to work, Electors must know *how* to choose—not be told *who* to choose. If the Electors are chosen by the people, then some process for nominating superior Elector candidates from whom the people can choose must be found.

> And this will be thought no inconsiderable recommendation of the constitution, by those, who are able to estimate the share, which the executive in every government must necessarily have in its good or ill administration. Though we cannot acquiesce in the political heresy of the poet who says—
>
> > "For forms of government let fools contest—
> > That which is best administered is best."

–yet we may safely pronounce, that the true test of a good government is its aptitude and tendency to produce a good administration.

This speaks to the strategy of the electoral process as designed in the Constitution. In other words get a good administration with good leaders time after time by the process rather than by politics or just plain luck.

The vice-president is to be chosen in the same manner with the president; with this difference, that the senate is to do, in respect to the former, what is to be done by the house of representatives, in respect to the latter.

Alexander Hamilton overstates his case here as the Senate will never make a selection unless there is a tie in the highest number of electoral votes after the President is chosen. *In every Case, after the Choice of the President, the Person having the greatest Number of Votes of the Electors shall be the Vice President.* (*US Constitution* Article II Section 1 Clause 3*)*

It should be noted that if the House of Representatives chooses a candidate on the list other than the one with the highest number of electoral votes, the one with the highest number of votes will become Vice-President. In other words, the person with the most electoral votes will either be President or Vice-President. Either way, we get a President and a Vice-President selected individually from the list of the best candidates the system could produce.

Hamilton continues:

The appointment of an extraordinary person, as vice-president, has been objected to as superfluous, if not mischievous. [Why would anyone object to having the second most qualified person in the nation as the vice-president?] It has been alledged, that it would have

> been preferable to have authorized the senate to elect out of their own body an officer, answering that description. But two considerations seem to justify the ideas of the convention in this respect. One is, that to secure at all times the possibility of a definite resolution of the body, it is necessary that the president [of the Senate] should have only a casting vote. And to take the senator of any state from his seat as senator, to place him in that of president of the senate, would be to exchange, in regard to the state from which he came, a constant for a contingent vote.

In other words, if a Senator were chosen as the President of the Senate he could only vote as a tie breaker rather than as a representative of his state. His state therefore would be under-represented. If one considers the Senators as just members of another body for passing national legislation, or as additional representatives of a political party, he would miss the critical nature of this argument.

> The other consideration is, that as the vice-president may occasionally become a substitute for the president, in the supreme executive magistracy, all the reasons, which recommend the mode of election prescribed for the one, apply with great, if not with equal, force to the manner of appointing the other. It is remarkable, that in this as in most other instances, the objection, which is made, would be against the constitution of this state. We have a Lieutenant Governor, chosen by the people at large, who presides in the senate, and is the constitutional substitute for the Governor in casualties similar to those, which would authorise the vice-president to exercise the authorities and discharge the duties of the president.

**PUBLIUS** (*Federalist No. 68*)

## No Political Parties Intended

Dr. W. Cleon Skousen in his book *The Making of America* mentions some assumptions upon which the electoral process was established:

> This entire procedure was set up on the assumption that there would be no political parties and that each state would submit the best candidates it could provide. In other words, it was expected that there would be many candidates. (*Making of America* p. 520)

The whole Electoral College System is based on the premise that all participants from those that choose the Electors, to the Electors themselves, to the members of the House of Representatives, have the interest of the nation as a whole as their primary concern.

# Version 2 – THE EVOLUTION

# Political Parties Rise to Power

Although the popular election of a president had been considered and rejected by the Framers during the Constitutional Convention,[39] the idea persisted among the people. The popular election of a president leads to a consolidated and often paternalistic government. The concept of addressing separate and conflicting interests in a way to satisfy both, gives way to accommodating only the will of the majority. In spite of the efforts of the Framers to construct the best method of electing a president and vice-president by a procedure that would not be subject to the sinister designs of scheming groups of men, this very phenomenon (which is characteristic of party-based parliamentary governments) began working its way into the new American government almost from the beginning. George Washington could see that it was happening. In his farewell address dated September 17, 1796,[40] Washington warned the country about the danger—but to no avail:

> I have already intimated to you the danger of Parties in the State, with particular reference to the founding of them on Geographical discriminations. Let me now take a more comprehensive view, and warn you in the most solemn manner against the baneful effects of the Spirit of Party, generally.

---

[39] According to Madison's Notes on July 17th George Mason, delegate from Virginia, put it this way:

[I]t would be as unnatural to refer the choice of a proper character for chief Magistrate to the people, as it would, to refer a trial of colours to a blind man. (*United States – Formation of the Union* p. 127)

[40] Washington's farewell address was first published September 19, 1796 in Philadelphia's *American Daily Advertiser.*

This spirit, unfortunately, is inseparable from our nature, having its root in the strongest passions of the human Mind. It exists under different shapes in all Governments, more or less stifled, controuled, or repressed; but, in those of the popular form it is seen in its greatest rankness and is truly their worst enemy.

The alternate domination of one faction over another, sharpened by the spirit of revenge natural to party dissension, which in different ages and countries has perpetrated the most horrid enormities, is itself a frightful despotism. But this leads at length to a more formal and permanent despotism. The disorders and miseries, which result, gradually incline the minds of men to seek security and repose in the absolute power of an Individual; and sooner or later the chief of some prevailing faction more able or more fortunate than his competitors, turns this disposition to the purposes of his own elevation on the ruins of Public Liberty.

Without looking forward to an extremity of this kind (which nevertheless ought not to be entirely out of sight) the common and continual mischiefs of the spirit of Party are sufficient to make it the interest and the duty of a wise People to discourage and restrain it.

It serves always to distract the Public Councils and enfeeble the Public administration. It agitates the Community with ill founded jealousies and false alarms, kindles the animosity of one part against another, foments occasionally riot and insurrection. It opens the door to foreign influence and corruption, which find a facilitated access to the government itself through the channels of party passions. Thus the policy and the will of one country are subjected to the policy and will of another.

There is an opinion that parties in free countries are useful checks upon the Administration of the Government and serve to keep alive the spirit of Liberty. This within certain limits is probably true, and in Governments of a Monarchical cast Patriotism may look with indulgence, if not with favour, upon the spirit of party. But in those of the popular character, in Governments purely elective, it is a spirit not to be encouraged. From their natural tendency, it is certain there will always be enough of that spirit for every salutary purpose. And there being constant danger of excess, the effort ought to be, by force of public opinion, to mitigate and assuage it. A fire not to be quenched; it demands a uniform vigilance to prevent its bursting into a flame, lest instead of warming it should consume. (*George Washington Collection* p. 519-520)

## The Spirit of Party

George Washington tells us that the spirit of party is a part of our nature, yet it ought to be kept under total control. So what part of our nature is it? It is the part that demonstrates itself in our biases and prejudices. These take the form of "*my gang is better than yours*" which is soon translated to "*my gang is right (or good) and yours is wrong (or evil).*" This is the basis first of pride, then of hate, and sows the seeds of war. The party mentality includes the win/lose philosophy which supposes that we need to contend with (and ultimately defeat) an enemy. After all, we are better than they are and can prove it with force. We all have biases and prejudices. To demonstrate this, just replace the word *gang* in one of the phrases with the word *team, neighborhood, high school, religion, race, nation, gender,* etc. The party systems of government are based on force and defeat of an enemy or at least the defeat of his position on a certain issue or bill. The spirit of party is the beginning of war. On the other hand, true freedom must be built on the spirit of peace and cooperation.

51

Communication is a major casualty of this win/lose paradigm. In their efforts to oppose other parties, members of one party quit listening to what is being said by anyone of another party except to gather ammunition for a rebuttal or some less noble purpose. The last thing a loyal party member would want to do is acknowledge any validity in the other party's point of view on any subject. Members of other parties are perceived as enemies and therefore must be considered evil and totally unworthy of any admiration or even respect. Candidates also don't want to be labeled as thinking like an opposing party on any topic. They therefore are forced to take the opposing view just to oppose–no matter what their position really would be if they were actually to analyze the situation prior to taking that stand. The contention between political parties only validates the statement that "the first casualty of war is truth." So essentially, in a government based on a party system, there is continually a state of low grade civil war. Is it any wonder that George Washington said that in popular governments the spirit of party "is seen in its greatest rankness and is truly their worst enemy"? Yet that was exactly what took place as presidential candidates deserted the candidate selection methodology specified in the Constitution (Electoral College System), and started to "run" for the presidency (popular vote system).

At first, political parties were not formalized and organized as they are today. They certainly would be considered special interests or factions. In the book *Life of Thomas Jefferson* by B.L. Rayner, which was originally published eight years after the death of Jefferson, the following passage affirms this baneful circumstance:

> Early in the year 1795, the two great parties of the nation became firmly arrayed against each other on the question of providing a successor to General Washington. Mr. Adams was taken up by the Federalists, and Mr. Jefferson was undividedly designated as the Democratic-Republican candidate.

The contest was conducted with great asperity. In fierceness and turbulence of character, in the temper and dispositions of the respective parties, and in the principles which were put in issue, the contest so strongly resembled those of which every generation since then has been eye-witnesses and actors as to render a description unnecessary. The issue was well-recognized. The struggle of the people against the party in power is always an unequal one, and was lost on this occasion. The majority, however, was inconsiderable. On counting the electoral votes in February, 1797, it appeared there were seventy-one for Mr. Adams and sixty-eight for Mr. Jefferson.[41]

## Electors Perceived to Make the Final Decision

Although the formality of the Electoral College nomination procedure was still being followed, the essential function of the system was quickly lost. The spirit of the constitutionally defined instruction which went to great lengths to make sure that Electors would be independent of government control and free from outside influence was totally ignored. Rather than relying upon the Electors to nominate the best individuals possible, the political factions were trying to use the Electors to force the final selection of their party's candidate. Making the final choice for President was not a constitutionally mandated prerogative of the Electors. In addition to this fact, nowhere in the Constitution were political factions or parties authorized or even mentioned. Since the nomination function of the Electors was being usurped by the political parties, there appeared to be no other purpose for the Electors to exist than to make the final choice of the President. Rather than being independent, the Electors had become pawns in a political party process.

---

[41] *Life of Thomas Jefferson* B. L. Rayner, edited by Eyler Robert Coates, Sr. (http://etext.virginia.edu/jefferson/biog/lj26.htm) - accessed 10/10/2010

## Evolution of the Nominating Function

Now that the Electors were perceived as the ones who were to make the final choice for President, a separate nominating function and narrowing down process evolved. For individuals pushing the election of a certain candidate for president, the option of having the election go to the House of Representatives was considered problematic and threatening. Instead of choosing someone as an Elector who would nominate wise candidates, Electors were chosen to support a certain candidate. The very individuals who were to be precluded from being Electors were influencing and controlling the Electors. At first this was done informally. Turning the nominating prerogative of the Electoral College openly over to the political parties followed afterwards.

Contrary to both the spirit and the actual words of the Constitution, both the Federalists (the more aristocratic faction) and the Republicans (the more democratic faction) were trying to manipulate the Electors. The issue was not whether the Electors were to be manipulated, it was who was to manipulate them. The movement toward the popular vote system not only soon annihilated the Federalist Party but also obscured the purpose of the Electoral College System for selecting presidents. In the party war that was taking place, the Constitution could be considered collateral damage.

The nomination function apparently was usurped first at the national level by so-called congressional caucuses, then moved to the state level. *World Book Encyclopedia*, referring to President Andrew Jackson, mentions the year 1828 as the year when "all nominations were made by state legislatures and mass meetings instead of by congressional caucuses." (*World Book Encyclopedia* vol. 11 p. 10) Mass meetings are now known as precinct caucuses and are held on local voting precinct levels. Whether considered on a national or a local level, the word *caucus*[42] is related to party activity. The nominating process wasn't assumed by the political parties until the second election of Andrew Jackson in 1832. According to the *World Book Encyclopedia*:

> [The] Election of 1832 was a milestone in American political history. For the first time, national political conventions chose the candidates for President. Before this time, the presidential candidates had been nominated by state legislatures, mass meetings, or congressional caucuses. (*World Book Encyclopedia* vol. 11 p. 12)

## Popular Election of Electors

As more and more of the states chose Electors by popular vote (see page 20), the process became more outcome based. Most people would not know who would be good at picking potential presidential candidates and therefore turned to their political parties to know who the parties wanted to win the presidency. They could then vote for the Electors who would support that candidate. This effectively opened the door for the people to vote for a president, albeit "indirectly", by voting for Electors who supported a certain presidential candidate.

## Popular Election of the President

To change from voting for an Elector who was committed to a certain candidate to having the presidential candidate's names on the ballots was an easy move. To say "electors for" on the ballot left little question in the voter's mind and avoided any research. Once the people get used to seeing the presidential candidates' names on the ballot, the "electors for" can be dropped.

---

[42] **CAUCUS**

A word used in America to denote a meeting of citizens to agree upon candidates to be proposed for election to offices, or to concert measures for supporting a party. The origin of the word is not ascertained. (*Noah Webster 1828*)

# Quality vs. Electability

Before we can adequately explain the differences in the results of using a party-based method of presidential election as opposed to the results of using the original Electoral College System for electing a president we must identify the goals of each. In a nutshell, the difference in the goals of the systems is between *quality* and *electability*. To find quality requires the application of correct principles. Electability, on the other hand, is based upon strategy—often using its less noble variety, stratagem (trickery or deceit).[43]

## The Quest for Quality

If your system only produces the best candidates, your system will always produce the best presidents. Of course this is true for all elected positions, but if we can sell the idea for choosing presidents the rest will follow.

The goal of the original electoral system is to locate the best qualified candidates possible. There is no win/lose issue with this electoral system. The best interest of the country is to find the most qualified President. The methodology is to choose the best individual from a field of the best candidates available. The old adage *the office should seek the man not the man seek the office* certainly applies to the original electoral system. That is exactly what the result of functioning in the constitutionally defined system would have been. Sadly, as a nation we did not stay on the high road, but rather yielded to our self-serving interests and reverted to the party methods and procedures so typical of mob rule.

---

[43] **STRATAGEM**
   1. An artifice, particularly in war; a plan or scheme for deceiving an enemy.
   2. An artifice; a trick by which some advantage is intended to be obtained.
      Those oft are *stratagems* which errors seem. (*Noah Webster 1828*)

In Noah Webster's *Examination of the Constitution*, dated October 10, 1787, he described the selection of the president as follows:

> The president of the United States is elective, and what is a capital improvement on the best governments, the mode of chusing him excludes the danger of faction and corruption.

Webster's *Examination of the Constitution* was put into pamphlet form and distributed. Noah Webster observed the same desertion of the founding principles that we have described. A note in Webster's own copy of his pamphlet includes the comment:

> This proves how little dependence can be placed on theory. Twelve years experience, or four elections demonstrates the contrary.

## The Issue of Electability

The party system operates on the premise that each party already considers itself better than the other parties, and therefore the most electable candidate from their party must be found. A party system is all about win/lose. The political parties soon learned that running multiple candidates from the same party is a recipe for losing the final election. The party system strategy is to narrow the field of candidates to one per party. The party that can get the most votes wins. To take the shortcut or the bypass in the selection for president, a plurality of votes is insufficient, a majority of the Electors must vote for a candidate. To get the vote of a majority of Electors in a party-based system a two party system is the only realistic alternative. The significant influence of additional parties would likely preclude obtaining a majority of Electors.

The obvious strategy from a party perspective is first to get Electors chosen from their party and then to influence those

Electors to "nominate" the predetermined party choice. This eliminates only part of the challenge. The big obstacle to a conversion to party rule (a democracy or simple republic) is the system outlined in the original Constitution. The Constitution requires each Elector to vote for two persons. That provision requires additional machinations from the parties to keep presidential candidates from opposing men of their own party.

The party solution to this dilemma was referred to as the "designation" principle, which is to say that one of the nominees was intended as a presidential candidate and the other as a vice-presidential candidate. Of course there is no such constitutional provision, but the idea readily caught on.

The next strategy that the parties resorted to was to team up presidential and vice-presidential candidates to garner votes from various parts of the nation and solidify support from various regional and ideological interests. The challenge for a party-based system superimposed upon the Electoral College System is to achieve party control over what should have been the prerogative of independent Electors. "Hijacking" (including ignoring, misinterpreting, and misusing the Constitution) is one way to accomplish this. Amending the Constitution is another alternative. Both were used.

## Nomination in the Party Context

We previously described nomination as the first naming of potential candidates. Originally the Electors' responsibility only pertained to nomination in this sense. In the context of the original electoral system, no other meaning would accomplish the goal of searching for the best possible candidates. In party politics, electability trumps quality. The emphasis is on electing someone who will promote the party agenda. There is a struggle within each party to come up with an electable candidate. The resolution of this conflict ends the intra-party contest and begins the inter-party contest.

Nomination at this stage in party politics is only the formal announcement of which candidate will run against candidates from opposing parties. At that point nominations are not dealing with naming the best possible candidates but with ending one contest and starting another. With that in mind, all aspects of an election are looked at in a very different light—a light that resembles the grim darkness of war! No wonder we talk about the lesser of two evils. How else could we describe a situation where the success of one side is measured in terms of the destruction and defeat of the other? We don't talk about high-quality candidates. We talk only of our candidate being better than the alternative.

## Evolution of the Role of the Electors

Having demonstrated how political party involvement undermined and subverted the whole design of the Electoral College System, let us now examine the actual changes that took place. As in all evolutionary changes to a system as opposed to intelligently designed modifications, the practice changed first. The changes afterward made to the Constitution tended to justify what was already happening rather than to provide direction to achieve well thought out purposes. To start our examination, we will look at the two presidential elections immediately following the administration of George Washington.

The year that the Electors are chosen is called a ***presidential election year.*** This is inaccurate. A more precise designation would be a ***presidential Elector selection year***. The counting of Electoral nominations (Phase 2) and the actual election of the president (Phase 3) take place the following year. This distinction is only significant if independently-thinking Electors each nominate the best potential candidates they can. If Electors are meeting to write down the names of predetermined candidates, it is only a technicality. Even though the expression is misleading, the elections are nearly always referred to this way; therefore, we will conform to the common terminology for this discussion.

## The Election of 1796

In the election of 1796 there were 138 Electors.  When the nominating votes of the Electors were counted (in 1797) John Adams was named President because a majority of the Electors had nominated him (the shortcut).  A majority of the Electors was 70.  John Adams received 71 electoral votes. Thomas Jefferson received 68 electoral votes.  This was the highest number of votes after the selection of the President and therefore Jefferson was Vice-President.  The nominees and the electoral votes for each were as follows:

| | |
|---|---|
| John Adams | 71 |
| Thomas Jefferson | 68 |
| Thomas Pinckney | 59 |
| Aaron Burr | 30 |
| Samuel Adams | 15 |
| Oliver Ellsworth | 11 |
| George Clinton | 7 |
| John Jay | 5 |
| James Iredell | 3 |
| George Washington | 2 |
| John Henry | 2 |
| Samuel Johnston | 2 |
| Charles C. Pinckney | 1 |

Unfortunately by 1796 the formation of parties[44] and party manipulation of Electors was evident.  As shown above, the nomination function of the Electors was still apparent.  The fact that there were 13 individuals named by the Electors shows that there were still some independent-thinking Electors.  One aspect of this system when applied in an evenly-divided party environment is that the likely result is a

---

[44] See page 52

president and a vice-president from opposing parties. That was the result of this election. The parties didn't like it.

## President/Vice-President Teams

By the next election the political factions or parties had increased their control and changed the whole complexion of the process. Instead of selecting Electors to suggest (nominate) the best candidates, as the electoral system was designed to do, the Electors were being chosen to support specific candidates previously selected by each party. In addition to this, the president/vice-president team concept was pushed by the parties. This effectively usurped the nominating function from the Electors and turned it over to the political parties. We consider this a serious breach of the Electors' constitutionally delegated responsibility. While this type of activity is very common among so-called "democratic" societies, it is contrary to the instruction in the Constitution.

In addition to giving the incumbent office holders a level of power approaching a political monopoly, it allowed the political parties to have excessive influence over the Electors and subsequently over the President who would be elected by them. This influence is contrary and repugnant to the intent of the Constitution. The whole direction of the system was evolving into a political battle destined to have all of the negative characteristics that the original system was designed to avoid. Allegiance to party interest became more important to the people than the principle of reconciling separate interests. Intrigue and corruption became the order of the day. Rumors and lies in the media as well as in personal communications were rampant. The whole electoral process was being perverted. The constitutional republic had become largely a representative democracy, subject to the demagoguery and deceit that goes along with rabble rousing.

# The Election of 1800

The election of 1800 caused the actual selection of the President to go to the House of Representatives. By now the idea that the election would go to the House under any circumstance was considered problematic by the political parties.[45] We maintain that it would have been a normal and common occurrence for the system as outlined in the original Constitution to put five candidates in the hands of the House for a selection. In fact, we believe that it would almost always have happened this way had the original system been maintained.

The electoral vote in this case ended in a tie with two candidates being nominated by a majority of the Electors. In the context of independent Electors, this seems statistically impossible. In a party context, or a president/vice-president team context, it would be probable.

## Counting the Electors' Votes

The certificates from the Electors were opened and tallied on Wednesday, February 11th 1801 in the Senate chambers. The declaration was made that there was a tie in electoral votes for the office of President. Thomas Jefferson and Aaron Burr each had received votes from a majority of the 138 Electors (276 votes total) and were tied with 73 votes each. This would

---

[45] Senator John Taylor from Virginia, who was in favor of the designation principle in the Senate debates of the 12th Amendment, did not want the election to ever go to the House. He put it this way:

> To have enlarged the number of nominees, would have increased the occurrence of an election by the House of Representatives; and if as I have endeavored to prove, it is for the interest of every state, that the election should be made by the popular principle of Government and not by that House, then it follows, that whatever would have a tendency to draw the election to that House, is against the interest of every State in the Union; and that every State in the Union is interested to avoid an enlargement of the nominees, if it would have such a tendency. (*The Founders' Constitution* vol. 5 p. 471)

have been extremely rare with independent Electors. What appears even more unlikely is that the tied candidates also belonged to the same political faction, (Democratic-Republican). Although the sitting Vice-President was one of the tied candidates, the sitting President was not. It seems rather odd that President John Adams would not have received more electoral nominations than the lesser known nominee, Aaron Burr. Of the remaining electoral votes, there were 65 for John Adams and 64 for Charles C. Pinckney. One vote was cast for John Jay. The electoral votes were as follows:

| | |
|---|---|
| Thomas Jefferson | 73 |
| Aaron Burr | 73 |
| John Adams | 65 |
| Charles C. Pinckney | 64 |
| John Jay | 1 |

Among 138 supposedly independent Electors there were only five nominees. This says that the Electors in the several states only found five individuals in the country worthy in their opinion of being President. No narrowing down of the field of candidates was necessary. It is obvious that the political parties had taken total control of the candidate selection process (Phase 2) as well as the nomination (Phase 1). It appears that the Federalists were smarter with their president/vice-president strategy than the Democratic-Republicans. Either the Republicans forgot to designate an Elector to vote for a different "vice-president" or the Elector forgot to do his "duty".

### The Election Goes to the House

The House of Representatives were responsible to decide between the tied candidates who had received the vote of a majority of the Electors. Even though everyone "knew" that Jefferson was the intended President and Burr the intended Vice-President, the Constitution didn't recognize such "knowledge". The process had to take its course. The

Constitution instructs the Electors to vote for two persons. Voting for two persons creates a field of candidates even if all Electors vote identically. It proves that the final selection was designed to be out of the Electors' control. If some of the Electors chose one candidate from their own state, as the Framers anticipated,[46] the likelihood of a tie would be greatly reduced. A tie is of no consequence unless a majority of the Electors nominate the same individuals. In their efforts to manipulate the Electors (in order to avoid a decision by the House), the political parties had unwittingly defeated their own purpose. The House was required to choose between the tied individuals.

"Immediately" as specified by the Constitution, the House of Representatives convened with the Senate present as witnesses. In the House there would be discussion, debate, and persuasion as the merits of the candidates were examined. Multiple ballots would be expected. Men would have to change their minds. To reach a concurrence of a majority of the states would require patient, convincing arguments and statesmanship. Unfortunately, when the spirit of party is strong, statesmanship is hard to find.

This tie situation was caused by party politics, the very thing that the Electoral College System was designed to avoid in the selection of the President. The House was divided along party lines with members of opposing parties making a choice between two Democratic-Republicans. Can anyone not be suspicious of "spoiler" motives on the part of the Federalists? They had no man of their party to vote for. The best they could hope for was to deny Jefferson the presidency by voting for Burr. At that time there were 16 states in the Union. A

---

[46] In Madison's Convention notes (Sept. 5) he quotes Gouverneur Morris: As each elector is to give two votes, more than ¼ will give a majority. Besides as one vote is to be given to a man out of the State, and as this vote will not be thrown away, ½ the votes will fall on characters eminent & generally known. (*United States – Formation of the Union* p. 669)

majority of the states (nine in this case) were needed to elect the President. On the first ballot, eight states voted for Jefferson, six states voted for Burr and two states, Maryland and Vermont were split. (Each had an even number of Representatives.) Jefferson had a plurality of half of the states, but a majority was required. As far as we can tell there was not much difference in the balloting for the first 35 ballots. No one was convinced to change his mind. Electing the best president took a back seat to partisan wrangling.

It actually took until Tuesday, February 17th on the 36th ballot to resolve the controversy. Those Representatives who had voted for Burr from the states that were split, Maryland and Vermont, abstained and Jefferson was elected. The South Carolina and Delaware delegations who previously had voted for Burr also abstained. The final vote was ten states for Jefferson, four states for Burr and two abstentions. Some people claim that those states that abstained would have reduced the total number of states for the count. We reject that argument outright. We claim that the intent of the Framers was that a majority of the states in the Union was needed and that number was nine.

Much of the credit for this final change of heart and concession is given to the efforts of Alexander Hamilton to convince some of his Federalist Party associates that even though there would be no necessity for them to cast their votes for Jefferson, he would be a better alternative than Burr; and that by just withholding their votes, the process would complete.

It appears that the whole of the House of Representatives had become more concerned with opposing those of the other party than fulfilling their duty to select the best of the candidates presented to them by the counting of electoral votes. We quoted Alexander Hamilton extensively as he, in *Federalist No. 68*, defended the process of selecting the chief executive. He showed that the design of the Electoral College

System was a way to avoid intrigue and cabal. As the Constitution (by ratification) turned from theory to practice, Mr. Hamilton was himself caught up in party politics. While we are grateful that he did rise to the occasion in 1801, and tried to convince his party to end their partisan opposition, that spirit of party had permeated the government and largely destroyed the integrity of the constitutional intent Hamilton had so ably defended in his attempt to get the Constitution ratified in the state of New York. The blight of party animosity would not only continue but would augment over the years.

# 12<sup>th</sup> Amendment Institutionalizes Party Usurpation

There are three ways to abuse (subvert) the Constitution:

a) Ignore it
b) Misinterpret it
c) Inappropriately amend it.

The Constitution can be inappropriately amended either by disregarding the technical instructions of amendment (Article V) or by amending it in such a way that the functionality is impaired—causing inconsistencies with other constitutional principles or provisions. The passage of the 12<sup>th</sup> Amendment did not violate specific instructions of how to amend. It did, however, circumvent the reason for establishing the Electoral College System.

Due to party influence and manipulation of the Electors relating to the selection of a President, the first two abuses had become commonplace. To sanction the first two abuses, the third was required.

## Amending the Constitution

Instead of recognizing their error in allowing the party system to usurp the Electors' constitutionally delegated responsibility of nominating presidential candidates, the now party-controlled Congress put together a bill to "fix" the "problem" in the Constitution. This "fix" was passed by Congress in December of 1803 and then hastily ratified by the states as the 12<sup>th</sup> Amendment (June 15, 1804). It reads as follows:

> The Electors shall meet in their respective states, and vote by ballot for President and Vice-President, one of whom, at least, shall not be an inhabitant of the same state with themselves; they shall name in their ballots the person voted for as President, and in

distinct ballots the person voted for as Vice-President, and they shall make distinct lists of all persons voted for as President, and of all persons voted for as Vice-President and of the number of votes for each, which lists they shall sign and certify, and transmit sealed to the seat of the government of the United States, directed to the President of the Senate;

The President of the Senate shall, in the presence of the Senate and House of Representatives, open all the certificates and the votes shall then be counted;

The person having the greatest Number of votes for President, shall be the President, if such number be a majority of the whole number of Electors appointed; and if no person have such majority, then from the persons having the highest numbers not exceeding three on the list of those voted for as President, the House of Representatives shall choose immediately, by ballot, the President. But in choosing the President, the votes shall be taken by states, the representation from each state having one vote; a quorum[47] for this purpose shall consist of a member or members from two-thirds of the states, and a majority of all the states shall be necessary to a choice. And if the House of Representatives shall not choose a President whenever the right of choice shall devolve upon them, before the fourth day of March next following, then the Vice-President shall act as President, as in the case of the death or other constitutional disability of the President.

The person having the greatest number of votes as Vice-President, shall be the Vice-President, if such

---

[47] **QUORUM**
  1. A bench of justices, or such a number of officers or members as is competent by law or constitution to transact business; as a quorum of the house of representatives. A constitutional *quorum* was not present.

number be a majority of the whole number of Electors appointed, and if no person have a majority, then from the two highest numbers on the list, the Senate shall choose the Vice-President; a quorum for the purpose shall consist of two-thirds of the whole number of Senators, and a majority of the whole number shall be necessary to a choice. But no person constitutionally ineligible to the office of President shall be eligible to that of Vice-President of the United States. (Amendment 12)

# Analyzing the 12<sup>th</sup> Amendment

At first glance, it appears that this would avoid the "problem" of pitting a president/vice-president team against each other in a run off in the House—but would not really change much else. We reject this argument as specious. Let us go through the amendment step by step and analyze it to show how the functions of the original system were obliterated by this amendment.

## *The Electors shall meet in their respective states*

The reason for meeting separately in their states was to avoid excessive pressure and outside influences on the Electors to vote a certain way (predetermined decisions).[48] We can see that by this time the process had been totally turned over to the outside influence of political parties and was all about predetermined decisions. This constitutional check now accomplishes absolutely nothing.

## *and vote by ballot for President and Vice-President,*

---

[48] Alexander Hamilton put it this way:
> And as the Electors, chosen in each state, are to assemble and vote in the State, in which they are chosen, this detached and divided situation will expose them much less to heats and ferments, which might be communicated from them to the people, than if they were all to be convened at one time, in one place. *(Federalist No.68)*

In the Senate debates on the 12th Amendment, Samuel White predicted that a separate vote for vice-president would only help the political parties get their presidential candidate into office. The character, merit, talents, and virtue of the man chosen as a vice-presidential candidate would not even be an issue. Said he:

> In this angry conflict of parties, against the heat and anxiety of this political warfare, the Vice Presidency will either be left to chance, or what will be much worse, prostituted to the basest purposes; character, talents, virtue, and merit, will not be sought after, in the candidate. The question will not be asked, is he capable? is he honest? But can he by his name, by his connexions, by his wealth, by his local situation, by his influence, or by his intrigues, best promote the election of a President? He will be made the mere stepping stone of ambition. (*The Founders' Constitution* vol. 5 p. 459)

The separate vote for presidential and vice-presidential candidates would only serve to get regional or other specific support for the party ticket rather than to select the best candidates for either office.

### *one of whom, at least, shall not be an inhabitant of the same state with themselves;*

The reason that the original system restricted each Elector to a maximum of one individual from their own state, was to avoid local bias and to get each Elector to look outside of his state for patriots—not to restrict naming potential presidential candidates from the same state (see page 27). The Framers considered a vote for a man of an Elector's own state as a vote "thrown away".[49] The process was now changed to where no real field of candidates for president was being made by the

---

[49] (see footnote 33 on page 35)

Electors. In fact, with one of each Elector's votes going to a vice-presidential candidate, the number of possible presidential candidates was cut in half. As far as nominations for president, the votes for vice-president were now "thrown away". There is no reason to have such a meaningless statement in the text of the Amendment. It appears to be there only to give the impression to the casual reader that nothing has changed much from the original design where a similar statement had purpose.

> *they shall name in their ballots the person voted for as President, and in distinct ballots the person voted for as Vice-President, and they shall make distinct lists of all persons voted for as President, and of all persons voted for as Vice-President and of the number of votes for each, which lists they shall sign and certify, and transmit sealed to the seat of the government of the United States, directed to the President of the Senate;*

This is just procedural, implementing the changes in concept. If we allow the possibility that the choice made by some Electors for President might be the choice of other Electors for Vice-President, this change drastically diminishes the odds of achieving a majority of electoral votes for either office—unless the Electors are mere pawns of the political parties.

> *The President of the Senate shall, in the presence of the Senate and House of Representatives, open all the certificates and the votes shall then be counted;*

The words are the same; the significance is gone. Instead of this counting of votes being the means of reducing the number of nominees to five or less candidates (Phase 2), this is now just a formality. The parties have already picked their candidates.

71

> *The person having the greatest Number of votes for*
> *President, shall be the President, if such number be*
> *a majority of the whole number of Electors*
> *appointed;*

This amendment effectively changed the Electors' function from *nomination* (Phase 1) to *final vote* (Phase 3) by using them to attempt to force the shortcut in *candidate selection* (Phase 2). This places the Electors in the position of being used as pawns to party machinations. Just think what it would do to the outcome if an Elector decided to reverse his vote for President and Vice-President just because he thought the individuals would do better in those respective roles. In order to achieve the goal of having the Electors choose the President and Vice-President, more collusion and manipulation would be required.

In the original version of the Electoral College System, the Electors each nominated two individuals. When the electoral votes were counted a field of candidates was created. If an individual met both of the following criteria, the field of candidates was reduced to one and the system would bypass the vote in the House:

a) One individual must have been nominated by more Electors than anyone else, and
b) Over half of the Electors must have nominated that individual.

The required majority to bypass the vote of the House was a majority of the number of Electors, not electoral votes. Since each Elector cast two votes, a candidate would need just over 25% of all electoral votes cast.

With the ratification of the 12th Amendment, it was impossible for two candidates to be tied with a majority of electoral votes because each Elector only casts one vote for President. While this solved the tie part of the "problem", obtaining the required majority became infinitely more difficult without abandoning the principle of independent Electors. For the shortcut to apply, a candidate would need over 50% of all electoral votes for President instead of over 25% of all electoral votes cast. This is the problem caused by the 12<sup>th</sup> Amendment "solution".

In theory, the Electors could act independently; but if a large number did so, the majority needed to bypass the vote in the House could not be achieved. In a vote by independent Electors, the election would always go to the House. The way to get around this would be manipulation of the Electors by the parties. The net effect of the 12<sup>th</sup> Amendment was to solidify party control of the nomination process.

The amendment continues:

> *and if no person have such majority, then from the persons having the highest numbers not exceeding three on the list of those voted for as President, the House of Representatives shall choose immediately, by ballot, the President. But in choosing the President, the votes shall be taken by states, the representation from each state having one vote; a quorum for this purpose shall consist of a member or members from two-thirds of the states, and a majority of all the states shall be necessary to a choice.*

Obviously the parties do not want the election for President to go to the House because parties work on the popular election concept. If the election goes to the House, the number of candidates for President is restricted to no more than three. This is of little consequence if the parties own the members of the House of Representatives. The party that controls the delegations from a majority of the states will prevail.

> *And if the House of Representatives shall not choose a President whenever the right of choice shall*

*devolve upon them, before the fourth day of March next following, then the Vice-President shall act as President, as in the case of the death or other constitutional disability of the President.*

This refers to the Vice-President elect as described next.

*The person having the greatest number of votes as Vice-President, shall be the Vice-President, if such number be a majority of the whole number of Electors appointed, and if no person have a majority, then from the two highest numbers on the list, the Senate shall choose the Vice-President; a quorum for the purpose shall consist of two-thirds of the whole number of Senators, and a majority of the whole number shall be necessary to a choice. But no person constitutionally ineligible to the office of President shall be eligible to that of Vice-President of the United States.*

The number of candidates for vice-president is restricted to two. The party with the most Senators wins unless you assume that some Senators will vote their conscience rather than follow their party affiliation (which option is becoming more and more remote).

## Opposition to the 12th Amendment

In examining the 1803 debate in the Senate concerning the 12th Amendment, we find that some of the Senators understood the electoral system as set up by Article II of the Constitution and were loath to change anything without a thorough study and analysis of the effects of those changes. Other Senators either did not understand the American constitutional paradigm as it relates to choosing the President, or had some interest in changing the system for their own ends.

74

Samuel White from Delaware in defending the original Constitution said, "we have not given it a fair experiment," and "we should be cautious how we touch it":

> What appears specious in theory, may prove very inconvenient and embarrassing in practice, and my objections go to any alteration of the Constitution at this time; we have not given it a fair experiment, and it augurs not well to the peace and happiness of the United States to see so much increasing discontent upon this subject, so many projected alterations to the great charter of our Union and our liberties; not less than four are now upon our tables, and which, if adopted, will materially change the most valuable features of the Constitution. ...
>
> ... Are we aware of what we are about? Is this the way in which the Constitution was formed? Was it put together with as much facility and as little reflection as we are tearing it to pieces? No, Mr. President, it was constructed after much thought, after long and mature deliberation, by the collected wisdom and patriotism of America, by such a set of men as I fear this country will never again see assembled; and we should be cautious how we touch it. (*The Founders' Constitution* vol. 5 p. 457)

William Plumer from New Hampshire pointed out that the original Constitution protects the interest of the small states:

> This amendment affects the relative interest and importance of the smaller States. The Constitution requires the Electors of each State to vote for two men, one of whom to be President of the United States. This affords a degree of security to the small States against the views and ambition of the large States. It gives them weight and influence in the choice. By destroying this complex mode of choice, and introducing the simple principle of designation,

the large States can with more ease elect their candidate. This amendment will enable the Electors from four States and a half to choose a President, against the will of the remaining twelve States and a half. Can such a change tend to conciliate and strengthen the Union? (*The Founders' Constitution* vol. 5 p. 462)

Samuel White also demonstrated how the political parties had taken over and controlled the Electors in opposition to the original intent. He indicated that under the proposed 12th Amendment, the choices would be effectively reduced to two (one from each party) and that would more than double the inducement for tampering with the Electors:

The United States are now divided, and will probably continue so, into two great political parties; whenever, under this amendment, a Presidential election shall come round, and the four rival candidates be proposed, two of them only will be voted for as President—one of these two must be the man; the chances in favor of each will be equal. Will not this increased probability of success afford more than double the inducement to those candidates, and their friends, to tamper with the Electors,   to exercise intrigue, bribery, and corruption, as in an election upon the present plan, where the whole four would be voted for alike, where the chances against each are as three to one, and it is totally uncertain which of the gentlemen may succeed to the high office? And there must, indeed, be a great scarcity of character in the United States, when, in so extensive and populous a country, four citizens cannot be found, either of them worthy even of the Chief Magistracy of the nation. (*The Founders' Constitution* vol. 5 p. 457)

Uriah Tracy from Connecticut explained the original plan corresponding to the workings of the Electors and the prerogatives of the House and Senate in this fashion:

> Let this statement of facts be kept in view while we examine the duties assigned by the Constitution to the several agents concerned. The duty of the Electors is precisely defined. They are each to bring forward two candidates fully qualified for President, because they cannot know at the time of giving their ballots upon which the choice will fall. The circumstance of two having a majority, and both being equal in number of votes, is an expression of the public will, through the only Constitutional organ, by which, in this case, the public will can be expressed, that both had the requisite qualifications. The public will, then, was in this instance clearly and unequivocally expressed, by a Constitutional and numerous majority, that both candidates were worthy of the office; but here the expression of the public will ceased, and which of these two should be President was now to be decided by another Constitutional organ, that is, by the House of Representatives, voting by states.
>
> The framers of the Constitution so intended, and the people who adopted it have so ordained, that their will in this case should be expressed by a majority of the states, acting by their representation in the House of Representatives. The right of selection is a right complete in itself, to be exercised by these second Electors, uninfluenced by any extraneous consideration, and governed only by their own sense of propriety and rectitude. The opinion of the people had been expressed by the Electors, but it only reached a certain point, and then was totally silent as to which of the two should be President, and their sense upon this point could only be collected through their Constitutional organ, the House of

Representatives, voting by states. Any interference of the first Electors, or of an individual or individuals, must be informal and improper. The advice of sensible and candid men, as in every other case, might be useful; but could have no binding force whatever. The first Electors had no right to choose a Vice President. To claim it was overstepping their duty, and arrogating to themselves a power not given to them by the Constitution.

If there is anything in this whole transaction which has the most distant appearance of a breach of duty, it was in the Electors, by attempting to designate, and by exercising the important office of an Elector under the influence of improper motives; that is, by officiously attempting to decide the question, which of the two persons was proper for Vice President, which they were constitutionally incompetent to decide. By this conduct they attempted to break down an important guard provided by the Constitution, and improperly to release themselves from its obligations, which made it their duty to select two men qualified to be President. (*The Founders' Constitution* vol. 5 p. 466)

Although the gentlemen mentioned above, along with others, made well-thought-out and well-delivered arguments for not hastily changing the Constitution, and demonstrated that the system was not "broken", in the end they did not prevail. The Amendment passed in the Senate and the House in a matter of days and was quickly ratified by the states in time for the 1804 election. We claim that with the ratification of the 12$^{th}$ Amendment, the electoral system is broken.

## The System is Still Broken

James Madison, in letters to Thomas Jefferson in 1824 and Henry Lee in 1825, demonstrates that the 12$^{th}$ Amendment did not seem to resolve the problems that were still apparent in the system. In their minds something else still needed changing.

To Thomas Jefferson, James Madison wrote:

> You have probably noticed that the manner in which the Constitution as it stands may operate in the approaching election of President, is multiplying projects for amending it. If Electoral districts, and an eventual decision by joint ballot of the two Houses of Congress could be established, it would, I think, be a real improvement, and as the smaller states would approve the one, and the larger the other, a spirit of compromise might adopt both. (*The Founders' Constitution* vol. 5 p. 472)

To Henry Lee, Madison said:

> In our complex system of polity, the public will, as a source of authority, may be the Will of the People as composing one nation; or the will of the States in their distinct & independent capacities; or the federal will as viewed, for example, thro' the Presidential Electors, representing in a certain proportion both the Nation & the States. If in the eventual choice of a President the same proportional rule had been preferred, a joint ballot by the two Houses of Congress would have been substituted for the mode which gives an equal vote to every State however unequal in size. As the Constitution stands, and is regarded as the result of a compromise between the larger & smaller States, giving to the latter the advantage in selecting a President from the Candidates, in consideration of the advantage possessed by the former in selecting the Candidates from the people, it cannot be denied whatever may be thought of the Constitutional provision, that there is, in making the eventual choice, no other controul on the votes to be given, whether by the representatives of the smaller or larger States, but

their attention to the views of their respective Constituents and their regard for the public good. (*The Founders' Constitution* vol. 5 pp. 472-473)

Twenty years after the 12th Amendment was ratified, they were still trying to figure out the proper method for electing a President. Additional amendments to the Constitution were being proposed and discussed. It appears that party influence was a given and proposals seemed to still address only "large state/small state" conflicts. Rather than trying to figure out how to return the designated function of the Electors, to find and nominate the best candidates, they seemed to be looking to see what was still wrong with the Constitution.

# Version 3 – THE DESTRUCTION

## The Electoral College Today
### Popular Election of the President

The ratification of the 12$^{th}$ Amendment opened the door to party control of the presidential election. This, in essence, legitimized tampering with and influencing Electors. The 12$^{th}$ Amendment mandated a separate vote for President and Vice-President—and made the process more closely match what was already being done. The changes made since the passage of the 12$^{th}$ Amendment have been more subtle. We haven't bothered to amend the Constitution; rather we have just chosen to ignore the intent while following the mechanics. One step at a time we have marched toward a popular vote based on campaigning. The Electoral College System was based on thoughtful consideration of merit by eminent Electors.[50] The popular election system requires candidates to appeal to the personal interest of the voters at the expense of the nation as a whole.

Today's version of the Electoral College, is a mere formality or rubber-stamp rather than a group of individuals that would determine anything. The Electors are each required to comply rather than to decide. Now we have totally replaced the Electoral College System with a popular vote system. The

---

[50] Alexander Hamilton uses the expression: "should be made by men most capable of analyzing the qualities adapted to the station" (*Federalist No. 68*—see page 29)

John Jay expresses it this way:
> As the select assemblies for choosing the President, as well as the State legislatures who appoint the senators, will in general be composed of the most enlightened and respectable citizens, there is reason to presume that their attention and their votes will be directed to those men only who have become the most distinguished by their abilities and virtue, and in whom the people perceive just grounds for confidence. (*Federalist No. 64*—see page 14)

popular vote system has retained an electoral-college facade to hold on to the appearance of conforming to the intent of the Constitution. Let us now describe how those important aspects of the Electoral College System were lost.

## No Independent Electors Allowed

Having achieved their ends in the election of president/vice-president teams and making the whole process subject to party rule (unofficially of course), the political parties continued to secure their stranglehold on American politics. In the first years following the ratification of the 12th Amendment, there is evidence that at least in theory, if not in practice, the concept of the intellectual independence of presidential Electors still prevailed. William Rawle demonstrates the discrepancy between theory and practice in this matter as early as 1829. He states:

> It must however be acknowledged that in no respect have the enlarged and profound views of those who framed the constitution, nor the expectations of the public when they adopted it, been so completely frustrated as in the practical operation of the system so far as relates to the independence of the Electors.

> It was supposed that the election of these two high officers would be committed to men not likely to be swayed by party or personal bias, who would act under no combination with others, and be subject neither to intimidation or corruption. ...

> ... experience has fully convinced us, that the Electors do not assemble in their several states for a free exercise of their own judgments, but for the purpose of electing the particular candidate who happens to be preferred by the predominant political party which has chosen those Electors. In some instances the principles on which they are chosen are so far

forgotten, that Electors publicly pledge themselves to vote for a particular individual, and thus the whole foundation of this elaborate system is destroyed. (*A View of the Constitution – Rawle* p. 57-58)

The Constitution carefully put checks in place to prevent the national government from influencing the outcome of the presidential nomination and election process. This is what Rawle's phrase *"the independence of the Electors"* refers to. Since political parties were not an official part of government, no checks could be put in place to protect against parties. The integrity of the people acting as individuals and groups would have to suffice. If the people were more interested in electing a particular politician than in maintaining a carefully designed system to provide statesmen for office time after time, the will of the people would prevail. If people were more determined to further only their own interest, at the expense of the interests of other individuals and groups, no legislation or constitution could change that tendency. The Framers only put checks in the Constitution that would control the government.[51] Judging from Mr. Rawle's quote, the nation abandoned constitutional principles for party politics soon after the Constitution was adopted.

The idea of an independent Elector actually pondering which individuals are most qualified to be President is so foreign to us today that it is not even considered an option. The nomination function of presidential candidates today has been entirely turned over to the political parties. The Electors' votes are now predetermined by the popular vote. What a farce! The current winner-take-all system awards the electoral votes of the state to the winner of the state popular vote. This effectively makes the presidency a prize to be won. The soldiers in this war are out to "capture" the White House.

---

[51] Key #8 of "15 Key Principles" states "The Constitution was designed to control the government, not to control the people" (see page 106) Explanation (www.freedomformula.us)

Neither the original Constitution nor the 12th Amendment authorizes a popular vote for President. Most Americans look at the electoral system as a hindrance to a popular vote. If the electoral vote goes contrary to the popular vote, they cry "foul!" and threaten to "fix" the problem by doing away with the Electoral College so that it will not interfere with the popular vote. Currently there is a movement called the National Popular Vote compact[52] designed to circumvent the Electoral College and to elect the President directly—without amending the Constitution. Several states have already passed laws that will award all of their state's electoral votes to whichever candidate wins the nation-wide popular vote.

The National Popular Vote compact (NPV) only changes the criterion for awarding the prize in each state. The popular vote totals in the nation are used rather than the popular vote totals from the state.

## The Two-Party System

It is often said that this nation was built on a two party system. There is no evidence in the Constitution of that. In fact there is no mention or reference to parties in the original Constitution. The closest things to parties mentioned in the Constitution are the states. Many of the colonists came from England where the Whigs and the Tories battled it out in a party system. It was only natural for them to superimpose the past on the evolution of the electoral system. At any rate, a two party system did become the de facto standard. Modifications to the system came first in practice, then by statute; and were designed to accommodate party politics.

---

[52] http://www.nationalpopularvote.com - accessed 10/10/2010
(see Appendix - page 99)

# Electors Pledged to a Candidate

As far as Electors publicly pledging themselves to a particular candidate, this is no longer considered outrageous as Mr. Rawle indicated. Now this is expected. Any Elector who dared vote for a different candidate than the party choice would be labeled a "faithless Elector." The use of this terminology actually makes it sound, if not illegal, at least immoral to vote his conscience! There are no national laws to prevent this, but 30 of the states have enacted laws to bind the presidential Electors to vote for the candidate of their party. Some go further: Oklahoma[53] and Washington[54] impose a civil penalty of up to $1,000; in North Carolina, the fine is $500.[55] In examining the state laws of Utah (where the authors resided when this book was written) we found the following:

> **20A-13-304. Meeting to ballot -- Casting ballot for person not nominated by elector's party.**
> (1) The electors shall meet at the office of the lieutenant governor at the state capitol at noon of the first Wednesday of the January after their election, or at noon of any other day designated by the Congress of the United States of America.
> (2) After convening, the electors shall perform their duties in conformity with the United States Constitution and laws.
> (3) Any elector who casts an electoral ballot for a person not nominated by the party of which he is an elector, except in the cases of death or felony conviction of a candidate, is considered to have resigned from the office of elector, his vote may not be recorded, and the remaining electors shall appoint another person to fill the vacancy.[56]

---

[53] Oklahoma Statutes 26-10-109
(http://www.oklegislature.gov/osStatuesTitle.aspx) – accessed 2/11/2013

[54] Washington Statutes RCW 29A.56.340
(http://apps.leg.wa.gov/rew/default.aspx?cite=29A.56.340) – accessed 2/11/2013

[55]http://www.ncsl.org/legislatures-elections/the-electoral-college.aspx#faithless – accessed 02/02/2013

Alabama handles the situation by having each Elector execute the following statement which is attached to the Elector's nomination by his or her political party:

> I do hereby consent and do hereby agree to serve as elector for President and Vice President of the United States, if elected to that position, and do hereby agree that, if so elected, I shall cast my ballot as such elector for _____ for President and _____ for Vice President of the United States[57]

The oath or pledge requirement for Oregon[58] is similar. New Mexico makes it a fourth degree felony to vote contrary to the commitment.[59]

It would appear, at least for the Electors, it has become illegal for any of them to think for themselves. They have become mere robots to confirm the outcome of the popular election for a president/vice-president team nominated and put into office by the demagoguery of a party machine. At least we don't execute or incarcerate the independent-thinking Elector for voting his conscience! The way the current system works, the few radical individuals in the few states that allow Electors to vote their conscience would not have any impact on the election anyway. Let us briefly recap how the electoral system works today.

---

[56] Utah Code 20A-13-304
(http://le.utah.gov/~code/TITLE20A/htm/20A13_030400.htm) - accessed 10/10/2010

[57] Code of Alabama Section 17-14-31
(http://www.legislature.state.al.us/codeofalabama/1975/coatoc.htm) – accessed 10/10/2010

[58] Oregon Revised Statutes 248.355
(http://www.leg.state.or.us/ors/248.html) – accessed 10/10/2010

[59] New Mexico statute 1-15-9
(http://www.conwaygreene.com/nmsu/lpext.dll?f=templates&fn=main-h.htm&2.0) - accessed 10/10/2010

## Electors Owned by Political Parties

Even though the Electors vote in their meeting in each state, no real decision is made by any individual Elector. The whole idea of voting is to make a choice and make it known what that choice is. This is true whether the vote is a nomination such as the original Electors made or a final election. Freedom depends upon free choice.[60]

The current practice is that those who want to "run" for president nominate themselves by announcing their intention—"throwing their hat in the ring", so to speak. Each political party determines from among those party members "running" for president who their candidate will be. This is done by campaigning, mudslinging, debates, primary elections and state and national party conventions, the very effects George Washington dreaded.[61] None of this rabble rousing has any basis in the instructions contained within the Constitution.

The vice-presidential candidate is chosen as a running mate by the party's candidate for president. The voters in the general election vote for a president/vice-president team. The results of the election are then superimposed back upon a system that makes it look like the Electors chose the president/vice-president team.

---

[60] Key #3 of "15 Key Principles" states: Freedom is the physical manifestation of agency and consequences, in the absence of coercion. (see page 106)
Explanation (www.freedomformula.us)

[61] Washington warned:
> The alternate domination of one faction over another, sharpened by the spirit of revenge natural to party dissension … sooner or later the chief of some prevailing faction more able or more fortunate than his competitors, turns this disposition to the purposes of his own elevation on the ruins of Public Liberty. (Washington's farewell address)

Within each state, each political party chooses their own slate of Electors. Each party therefore has a separate set of Electors who will "vote for" their president/vice-president candidate team if that team wins the statewide popular vote.[62] The Electors in this regard provide only a formal confirmation (rubber-stamp) of the outcome of the popular election which everyone already knows. The media blasts the results around the world before the polls even close on election day.

---

[62] Maine and Nebraska differ slightly, but the result is still determined by popular vote. (see page 92)

# Original Intent vs. Evolution and Destruction

Now let us review the biggest differences between the Electoral College System as it was intended under the original design of the Constitution compared to how the popular vote system functions today. While we preface our description of the current version with the word *now*, the tactics being used go back in many cases to the time of the 12th Amendment and before.

Originally:

> The purpose of the Electors was to nominate well-qualified *possible* presidential candidates. In fact the system was designed to provide the best potential candidates. The Electors were to start the candidate selection process by each nominating two outstanding individuals.

Now:

> The Electors perform only a rote mechanical process— weeks after the President has "won" the election. There is no need for real people to be involved. This is just a statistical derivative.

Originally:

> The tabulation of the nominations created a field of candidates. Normally the field would consist of five candidates—those with the highest number of nominating electoral votes. The final choice in this situation would have been made by the House of Representatives. Each state would have one vote— regardless of the number of Representatives from that state. To elect a President, a majority of the states needed to concur.

Now:

> The counting of the electoral votes is totally ritualistic. Nothing new is revealed to anyone. The outcome of the

election is already known. Both the nomination and candidate selection functions are now performed by the political parties and are usually accompanied with arguing, wrangling, and political maneuvering.

Originally:

The President and Vice-President would both come from the same pool of up to five candidates formed from counting the electoral votes. The Electors, acting independently, were not to have any control over which candidate might become President. They were to submit the names of the best nominees they could find.

Now:

The presidential candidates from each party select a "running mate" who will garner votes for the team. The criteria for selection is often that the vice-presidential candidate can obtain votes from a different geographic area and political position, such as bring more liberals, moderates, or conservatives to vote for the team. The individual selected as the vice-presidential candidate is sometimes one of the same candidates that the presidential candidate spoke so disparagingly about in the party campaigning process.

Originally:

The system was designed as a win-win selection of the best candidates possible. The Electors were to nominate eminent statesmen rather than popular party politicians.

Now:

Even before the acclaimed "grassroots" citizens get involved, supporters of each candidate build party machines to elect their candidate and disparage all other contenders in their own party. After securing their party's endorsement, they then unite in a greater hatred—the opposing party. All their efforts are focused on defeating the other party's candidate. Electability becomes more important than principles or the capability of the candidates.

Originally:

The system was designed to elect the President without campaigning and demagoguery. Candidates would be selected on the basis of the value or service they had previously provided to their state or to the nation—past performance rather than campaign promises.

Now:

The system is all about campaigning and campaign funding—spending billions of dollars and campaigning for years. This leads to the campaign promises that very closely resemble bribery and usually imply a more than constitutional presidential involvement in the legislative process. In other words, the executive campaigns on his agenda and ability to pass certain legislation. Legislation is not a constitutional presidential prerogative. This campaigning encourages paternalism and central government solutions to local problems.

Originally:

The election of members of the U.S. House of Representatives and the appointment of U.S. Senators by the states were separate from the appointment of Electors. The states originally set the time to appoint Senators and elect Representatives; therefore there were no coat-tail elections.

Now:

The whole election process is party oriented and party controlled.

Originally:

> It was entirely up to each state legislature how qualified presidential Electors were to be appointed. The Constitution has not been changed in that regard. The Constitution specified several protections to prevent Electors from being unduly pressured or influenced to choose certain individuals.

Now:

> The state legislatures have turned this responsibility over to the political parties. Each Elector must be committed to his party and specifically to the party's presidential candidate before he can be an Elector. In practice the political parties select the Electors either by party leadership or in party conventions. Each party submits the names of their Electors to the state. The party winning the presidential vote in the state supplies its Electors for a pre-committed outcome.

Originally:

> The Electors for a state could have a split vote. Considering the fact that two names were required from each Elector, it was always a split vote prior to the 12th Amendment. With all Electors doing their own thinking, it was possible for each state to nominate many potential candidates.

Now:

> Except in Maine and Nebraska, all electoral votes are awarded to the president/vice-president team that receives the most popular votes in the state.[63] This is known as the winner-take-all system. In Maine and Nebraska each congressional district has one electoral vote awarded to the slate of candidates with the most

---

[63] Those states with National Popular Vote compact law will award the electoral votes for their state to the candidates winning the national popular vote. (see Appendix - page 99)

popular votes in that district. The remaining two electoral votes go to the winner of the state-wide popular vote.

Originally:

The presidential candidates could not even be determined until the certified lists from the Electoral College meetings were opened by the President of the Senate and the votes were tallied. The Vice-President was selected from the same pool of candidates and could only be determined after the President was chosen.

Now:

The news media broadcasts every few minutes how many electoral votes each president/vice-president team has captured, even before the voting in a state is complete. Hours before the polls close in the western states, the election results are announced by the media. The actual meeting to open and officially tally the electoral votes is only a formality. The whole world already knows the outcome—and has since election day.

Originally:

The structure of the United States government was a complex representative republic. One of the distinguishing features was indirect election of some positions to represent different interests. This was effectively exhibited by the indirect method of selecting Presidents.

Now:

After the destruction of the original Electoral College System it has become largely a representative democracy, (popular vote system) subject to the demagoguery and deceit that goes along with rabble rousing.

93

| Original Electoral College System | Now – Party Popular Vote |
|---|---|
| Indirect multi-step method | Direct popular vote (not authorized by Constitution) |
| Complex representative republic | Representative democracy |
| Protects separate interests | Promotes personal interests only |
| Electors 1$^{st}$ step in the process | Electors last step—rubber-stamp |
| Competent Electors each nominate 2 outstanding statesmen Same day in every State | Self-nominate—or picked by a few political party elites States vie to be first in Primaries |
| Independent Electors ponder most qualified on past service & merits | Party owns Electors—pre-committed —no thinking allowed |
| No Campaigning —office seeks the man —not men seek the office | Candidates Campaign for years —to capture the White House <ul><li>Promises</li><li>Party platform</li><li>Legislative agenda (not a presidential prerogative)</li><li>Fixing the economy (not a presidential prerogative)</li><li>Appeal to emotions and whims—bribing</li><li>Raise millions of dollars</li><li>Promote other politicians (coat tail elections)</li></ul> |
| Protects Constitutional Federalism | Institutes consolidated party-run government by destroying the checks and balances |
| Safeguards the interest of the nation as a whole | Promotes personal dependence and entitlement attitude |
| Tallying the certified lists creates a field of candidates | Opening the certificates is only a superficial ritual |
| House chooses from the 5 highest States equal vote in final election Majority of States required for final choice (Small States have a voice) | Parties do not want the States to choose the President |
| President and Vice-President both from 5 most outstanding persons Vice-President highest electoral vote after the President chosen | Political parties nominate the presidential candidate Presidential candidate picks team-mate to win the most votes |
| President of the Union of States | King of the people—Legislator in chief |

# Conclusions

What seems like a small change in the beginning can have large consequences when allowed to go to fruition. The movement of only a few inches of a railroad track at a switch can cause a train to go a completely different direction. What seem like small and insignificant changes to the Electoral College System have us operating under a completely different paradigm than the Framers of the Constitution designed.

The original system outlined in the Constitution was a system built around independent Electors. The evolution of the Electoral College System gave us manipulated Electors. We now have rubber-stamp Electors owned by the political parties and obligated to vote for a president/vice-president team that won their state's popular election. Direct election of the President is not authorized by the Constitution.

For years there has been talk of eliminating the Electoral College and going to a strictly popular vote system for President. The philosophy, "one person one vote" appeals to the uninformed masses and those who want to gain personally by electing a particular candidate. The national interest and the state interests however are disregarded. Even in its ashes the existence of the Electoral College serves as a reminder of the plan of the Framers to create a system of Constitutional Federalism. As a check to the popular vote system, the Electoral College protects the less populous states from being totally bullied by the population centers not only in the selection of a President but in the administration and legislation enacted by individuals elected in this manner.

The current National Popular Vote movement attempts to bypass the Electoral College without a constitutional amendment. Essentially this movement would replace the state popular vote winner-take-all system with a national popular vote winner-take-all system. Bypassing is easy; we have been ignoring the Constitution for over two centuries. What is really needed is a return to constitutional principles.

Reacting to many usurpations of the national government, many states are currently trying to figure out how to reclaim their constitutional prerogatives through back-door approaches such as nullification. At first glance this seems like a logical solution. As we examine specious solutions such as nullification we come to the conclusion that, to use the vernacular, if the front door were not broken we wouldn't be so intent on the using the back door. Why not fix the front door? The Constitution was designed to recognize and protect separate and sometimes conflicting interests.[64] Arguably, the prime example of this was the mode of electing Presidents which we have outlined in this book. The rise to power of political parties was behind the evolution and destruction of that great system.

We advocate a return to the plan of the Framers to get the best presidential candidates possible. Our enemy here is not the national government or even the "other" party. It is the spirit of party that must prevail in a party based system. Earlier we quoted from George Washington's farewell address as he warned us of the spirit of party. A brief excerpt in summary:

> This spirit, unfortunately, is inseparable from our nature, having its root in the strongest passions of the human Mind. It exists under different shapes in all Governments, more or less stifled, controuled, or repressed; but, in those of the popular form it is seen in its greatest rankness and is truly their worst enemy.
>
> … the common and continual mischiefs of the spirit of Party are sufficient to make it the interest and the duty of a wise People to discourage and restrain it.[65]

---

[64] Key #10 (see "15 Key Principles" page 106)
Explanation (www.freedomformula.us)

We need to recognize blind allegiance to political parties as a problem rather than rely on that allegiance as a solution. That does not mean that we can not be associated with a party. It means that the party does not control our thinking or our voting. We need to become independent thinkers and voters rather than sheep. We as individuals must be willing to take the effort to examine the motives, actions, proposals, thinking and direction of our elected officials at all levels. We must be willing to vote for someone of another party, if that individual more closely adheres to the principles we believe in.

This is where education in "the science of government" becomes so vital. When the people are ready to learn about freedom and what made this nation great, they will see that freedom is more important than allegiance to political party. The biggest obstacle to restoring the original Constitution is the adherence to the party system that supplanted it so early in our history.

Once we as individuals have decided and committed to stand up for freedom, the next step is to get our friends and neighbors to do the same. After these two steps have been taken, it is time to fill our state legislatures with statesmen rather than politicians. State and local governments are only the product of our individual commitment. If we are willing to let things go on as they are, state and local governments will continue in the mode they now pursue. As long as our state legislatures are composed of political party pawns the suggestions that follow are not really viable.

With respect to presidential elections, the state legislatures do not need to leave the process in the hands of the political parties. It would take courage and statesmanship but they could reclaim their prerogative and control over presidential elections by returning to the principles of the original Constitution.

---

[65] Washington's farewell address was first published September 19, 1796 in Philadelphia's *American Daily Advertiser.*

One constitutionally authorized action that state legislatures could take would be to restore the nominating function of the Electoral College System. Instead of letting the parties choose the presidential candidates, each state could change their election laws to conform to the intent of the original Constitution. The Legislatures of each state have complete authority and control over the manner and method of appointing the Electors for their state. Election processes could be established that would select independent Electors. Wise men and women could be found to nominate outstanding individuals as potential candidates for President according to the plan described in the original Constitution.

In our opinion, having wise Electors nominate the most qualified presidential candidates is the way to go. The best answer by far is to return to the original design of the Framers as carefully outlined in Article II of the Constitution.

# Appendix

## National Popular Vote

Having studied this book, and realizing that the most important function of the Electors was to nominate outstanding potential candidates rather than to rubber-stamp the results of a popular vote, the reader should readily see that the following plan is a another step in the wrong direction. ***This popular movement to bypass the Electoral College will not result in electing better presidents.***

From their official website www.nationalpopularvote.com:[66]

> The National Popular Vote bill would reform the Electoral College by guaranteeing the Presidency to the presidential candidate who receives the most popular votes in all 50 states (and the District of Columbia). The bill would enact the proposed interstate compact entitled the "Agreement Among the States to Elect the President by National Popular Vote." The compact would take effect only when enacted, in identical form, by states possessing a majority of the membership of the Electoral College (that is 270 of the 538 electoral votes). Under the compact, all of the members of the Electoral College from all states belonging to the compact would be from the same political party as the winner of nationwide popular vote. Thus, the presidential candidate who receives the most popular votes in all 50 states (and the District of Columbia) will be guaranteed a majority of the Electoral College, and hence the Presidency. ...the compact has the additional benefit of eliminating the possibility that a presidential election might be thrown into the U.S. House of Representatives (with each state casting one vote).

---

[66] Accessed 10/10/2010

All 50 states and the District of Columbia have introduced bills to modify the election process. The goal is to circumvent any remaining functionality of the Electoral College and elect the President directly without amending the Constitution. The method is to force the Electoral College to reflect the national popular vote.

As of February 2013:

> Eight states and the District of Columbia have enacted the National Popular Vote agreement.[67] Their electoral votes total 132. The states are:
>> Vermont (3), California (55), Hawaii (4), Illinois (20), Maryland (10), Massachusetts (11), New Jersey (14), and Washington (12)

In our discussions with people concerning The National Popular Vote compact (NPV), we see some enthusiastically predicting it will restore "fairness" to the U.S. presidential elections while others say that it will be a disaster to the political future and well-being of the less populous states. Our opinion is that neither of these positions is accurate.

NPV is the last step in the evolutionary march from a complex constitutional representative republic that promotes freedom, to a simple republic that promotes democracy under political party control.

The Electoral College has already been reduced from the nomination process for statesmen to a statistical representation of the outcome of each state's popular vote for president. To make it reflect the outcome of the nation's popular vote instead—is no big deal.

We ask ourselves: "What is the outcome if NPV is defeated?" Our answer, we travel no further down the wrong road—the road leading away from the intelligent design of the Framers.

---

[67] www.nationalpopularvote.com – accessed 02/11/2013

This however does not reverse the evolution, abuse, and destruction of the Framers' plan that has already taken place. In order to reestablish freedom, there must be a return to the founding principles of the nation.

On the other hand, the worst consequence of implementing NPV would be that without the threat of a potential exception to the President always being elected by strict popular vote, no longer would people ask the question, "Why did the Framers establish the Electoral College?" Therefore the original Electoral College would become no more than a relic of an ingenious political system designed to establish and maintain freedom—lost in history.

Whether NPV passes or not, does nothing to release the stranglehold that the political parties have on elections and every other aspect of government operations. The candidates will still be political party pawns. As long as we have to choose between the lesser of two evils, the purposes and benefits of the original Electoral College will always remain hidden.

In this book we have shown the evolution and destruction of the Framers ingenious plan to elect the best Presidents. The National Popular Vote compact (NPV) could be considered the *coup de grâce* to a system that is all but gone.

# Election Date Requirements

## 1789 Election Dates

| Event | Determination of Date | Date |
|-------|----------------------|------|
| Appoint Electors | First Wednesday in Jan. | Jan. 7 |
| Electors Vote | First Wednesday in Feb. | Feb. 4 |
| Count Electors' Votes | | Apr. 6 |

## 1792 Election Dates

| Event | Determination of Date | Earliest | Latest |
|-------|----------------------|----------|--------|
| Appoint Electors | Within 34 days prior To Electors' vote. Every 4$^{th}$ year | Oct. 28 | Nov. 30 |
| Electors Vote | First Wednesday in Dec. After appointment | Dec. 1 | Dec. 7 |
| Count Electors' Votes | Second Wed. in Feb. | Feb. 8 | Feb. 14 |

## Current Election Dates

| Event | Determination of Date | Earliest | Latest |
|-------|----------------------|----------|--------|
| Electors from Winning Party "Appointed" | Tuesday next after first Monday in Nov. Every $4^{th}$ year | Nov. 2 | Nov. 8 |
| Electors Vote | Monday after second Wednesday in Dec. After appointment | Dec. 13 | Dec. 19 |
| Count Electors' Votes | $6^{th}$ day of Jan. 1:00 pm | Jan. 6 | Jan. 6 |

# Explanation of References

***Documentary History of the First Federal Elections – Vol. 1***
Jensen, Merrill and Becker, Robert A. ed. *The
Documentary History of the First Federal Elections 1788-
1790.* University of Wisconsin Press, 1976.
ISBN 0-299-06690

***Documentary History of the First Federal Elections – Vol. 3***
DenBoer, Gordon ed. *The Documentary History of the
First Federal Elections 1788-1790.* University of
Wisconsin Press, 1986.
ISBN 0-299-06690 (vol. 1)

***Examination of the Constitution***
Webster, Noah. *An Examination into the Leading
Principles of the Federal Constitution Proposed by the
late Convention held at Philadelphia.* Philadelphia:
Prichard & Hall
Reprinted from Webster's own copy  by Paul Leicester
Ford in *Pamphlets on the Constitution of the United States*

***Federalist***
Wills, Garry, ed. *The Federalist Papers.* by Alexander
Hamilton, James Madison and John Jay. Bantam, 1982.
ISBN 0-553-21340-7

***The Founders' Constitution***
Kurland, Philip B. and Lerner, Ralph, ed. *The Founders'
Constitution.* Indianapolis: Liberty Fund,
Originally published Chicago: University of Chicago
Press 1987.

***George Washington Collection***
Allen, W. B. ed. *George Washington, a Collection*
Indianapolis: Liberty Fund, 1988.
ISBN 0-86597-060-2

***Making of America***

Skousen, W. Cleon. *The Making of America.* Second Edition. Washington DC: The National Center for Constitutional Studies, 1986.
ISBN 0-88080-017-8

***Noah Webster 1828***

Webster, Noah. *An American Dictionary of the English Language.* Facsimile Edition published by the Foundation for American Christian Education.
ISBN 978-0-912498-03-4
Originally published New York: S. Converse, 1828.

***A View of the Constitution – Rawle***

Rawle, William. *A View of the Constitution of the United States of America*
2nd Ed. Reprinted by The Confederate Reprint Company 1998.
Originally published Philadelphia: Philip H. Nicklin, Law Bookseller, 1829.

***United States – Formation of the Union***

*Documents Illustrative of the Formation of the Union of the American States.*
69th Congress, 1st Session. Washington DC: Government Printing Office, 1927.

***World Book Encyclopedia***

*World Book Encyclopedia.* 1990.

# 15 Key Principles

*Keys to Understanding the*
*Paradigm of the Founding Fathers*

1. God is the source of all truth.

2. God is the source of freedom.

3. Freedom is the physical manifestation of agency and consequences, in the absence of coercion.

4. Justice is the absence of injustice; it is achieved by securing individual rights.

5. Natural Law, or God's Law, should be the foundation of municipal law.

6. Religion, morality, and knowledge in the science of government are the pillars of human happiness and political prosperity.

7. The Declaration of Independence declares the principles of freedom; the United States Constitution is the strategy for freedom.

8. The Constitution was designed to control the government, **not** to control the people.

9. The national government was to deal with the states and other nations; the states and local governments were to deal with the people.

10. The Constitution was structured to recognize and protect separate and sometimes conflicting interests.

11. The *Formula for Freedom* is found in the structure of the United States Constitution:

    Limited, delegated powers. (Enumeration)
    Vertical distribution of powers. (Federalism)
    Horizontal separation of powers. (Separation)
    Checks. (Bridle usurpation)
    Balances. (Representation of all interests)
    Secured rights. (Individual sovereignty)

12. The Framers intelligently designed The United States of America to be a complex constitutional representative Republic **not** a Democracy.

13. The first 10 amendments, The Bill of (individual) Rights, do not amend the original intent of the Constitution. They clarify the restraints placed on the national government and they safeguard the rights of individuals.

14. The 9th and 10th Amendments are the keystones to preserving Freedom.

15. In order to retain the divinely inspired Constitution, the "Miracle at Philadelphia," every generation must be educated in the divine science of government and be vigilant in its preservation.

### Advance Freedom, LLC

*The American Constitutional Paradigm* ™
*www.freedomformula.us*

# Test Your Knowledge of These Critical Concepts

Why did the Framers incorporate indirect elections in the Electoral College System process of selecting presidents for the United States? (see pages 12-17, 28-33)

Why did the Framers reject the idea of a direct popular vote for president? (see pages 13, 29, 49)

How many national offices did the original Constitution authorize people to vote for directly? (see page 12)

Why was it important that the Electors not hold office or be employees of the national government? (see pages 21, 29-33)

Why is it important that the Electors be independent of any obligation to outside influence groups, lobbyists, factions, etc? (see pages 21, 77-78)

In the original design, how were electoral votes actually nominating votes? (see pages 23-24)

Why was it important that the states have a voice in the selection of Electors as well as an equal vote in the final choice for president? (see pages 17-18, 41, 77)

Why do the authors say that political parties precipitated the destruction of the electoral system? (see pages 49-53)

Why do the authors say that the 12th Amendment institutionalized party usurpation? (see page 67)

# Index

utilizes indirect election & direct election, 12, 13, 77
Constitutional Federalism, 8, 18, 20, 40, 41, 42, 95
Democracy
  direct elections, 12, 15
  does not protect freedom, 2, 13
  does not protect interests of minority, 49
  evils of, 13
  popular vote, 15, 49, 81, 83, 84, 89, 93, 95, 99, 100
  simple republic, 8, 9, 15, 58, 61, 93, 100
  spectacles of turbulence and contention, 2, 30, 53
Democratic-Republican Party, 52, 54, 63, 64
Elector
  - constitutional specification, 17
    national government employee precluded, 10, 32
    national government officer precluded, 10, 32
    Senators and Representatives precluded, 10, 20, 22, 32
  - definition, 7, 9
  -1 originally
    duties
      each nominates 2 individuals, 22, 24, 26, 27, 33, 34,
        58, 72, 89
      each Elector independent, 24, 36, 40, 42, 43, 44, 53, 95
  -2 evolution
    duties
      each nominates 1 individual for president, 67
      each nominates 1 individual for vice-president, 67
      nominates no more than 1 from his own state, 70
    manipulated by political parties, 61, 95
  -3 now
    duties
      rubber-stamp state popular vote, 5, 81, 88, 89, 95, 99
      vote for predetermined party choice, 85, 86
        faithless Elector, 85
    owned by political parties, 82
Electoral College
  - definition, 7
  difference between US Electoral College and all others, 10
  term electoral college not used by the Framers, 9

wanted a bi-cameral congress, 12, 13, 14, 15, 20
were overly optimistic expecting a concensus of
    nominations, 43
Freedom
    built on spirit of peace and cooperation, 51
    democracy does not protect freedom, 13
    depends upon free choice, 87
    more important than party allegiance, 97
Gerry, Elbridge
    - delegate to Constitutional Convention, 13
    excesses of democracy, 13
    people are easily misled, 13
Hamilton, Alexander
    - delegate to Constituional Convention, 28
    caught up in party politics, 66
    defends the Electoral College System, 28–46
    Electoral College avoids intrigue and cabal, 31, 43, 44
    Federalist No. 68, 28–46, 65
    Federalist Party, 65
    less than majority of Electors not conclusive, 43
    preliminary selection (nomination), 29
House of Representatives
    direct election
        members popularly elected, 13
    national interest of the people, 14
House of Representatives - Electoral System Duties
    choose between tied candidates, 63
    choose from up to 5 candidates, 39, 40
    deciding vote bypassed, 16, 38
    each state has 1 vote, 42, 43, 77, 89
    majority of states necessary to a choice, 41, 68
    normally elect the president, 16, 22, 24, 35, 43
    present when certificates opened, 35, 68
Indirect vs. Direct Election
    - direct election - by all voters, 15
    - indirect election - by delegates, 12, 15
    Articles of Confederation indirect only, 12
    House members direct election represent the people, 13

# Share the Principles of Freedom
With Family, Friends, and Colleagues


CHECK YOUR LEADING BOOKSTORE,
AMAZON.COM
or:

**To order additional copies:**


## *The Evolution and Destruction*
### *of the*
# *Original Electoral College*


$11.95 + $3.00 shipping
Quantity discounts available

Order on line:  www.freedomformula.us
Or email:      books@freedomformula.us
Or call:       801-599-9819

➜ Coming soon: new books by Gary & Carolyn Alder

*The Evolution and Destruction of Constitutional Federalism*

*The Quest for Freedom*
*—In Search of the American Constitutional Paradigm*

For an in-depth study of the United States Constitution, the paradigm
of the Founders, and the principles of freedom in the religious,
economic, and political realms visit our website:
***www.freedomformula.us***

119

66103891R00075

Made in the USA
Middletown, DE
05 September 2019